# My Mediterranean Gardens

~

*Practical Personal Essays*

Barbara Jean Euser

WRITERS' WORKSHOPS
INTERNATIONAL

Copyright © 2021 by Barbara Jean Euser
All rights reserved

For permission to reprint essays, please contact
the author at bjeuser@yahoo.com

Published by
Writers' Workshops International
3465 County Road 23
Fort Lupton, Colorado 80621
United States of America

Library of Congress Control Number: 2020922699

**Cataloging Data**

Gardening – California
Gardening – Mediterranean
Gardening – Greece
Habitat Gardening
Native Plants – California
Bee Keeping
Medicinal Plants
Chinese Medicinal Plants
Plant Lore
Herbs
Low-water Gardening

ISBN: 978-0-9842992-2-5

Cover Illustrations by Dimitris Delacovias
Interior Design by Dianne Nelson

Printed in the United States of America

# Contents

~

### Chapter One: Birds and Bees

Blooms to Attract Hummingbirds . . . . . . . . . . . 2
LuAnn's Garden . . . . . . . . . . . . . . . . . 6
Sustainable Gardening . . . . . . . . . . . . . . . 9
How to Help Our Pollinators. . . . . . . . . . . . . 13
Beginning Beekeeping . . . . . . . . . . . . . . . 17
Backyard Beekeeping . . . . . . . . . . . . . . . 20

### Chapter Two: Flowering Herbs

Rosemary Means Remembrance. . . . . . . . . . . . 24
Long-lasting Lavender . . . . . . . . . . . . . . . 27
Achilleas: Legends and Lore . . . . . . . . . . . . 31
Superlative Salvias . . . . . . . . . . . . . . . . 35
Lemon Verbena . . . . . . . . . . . . . . . . . 39
It's About Thyme . . . . . . . . . . . . . . . . . 42
Chinese Garden Herbs . . . . . . . . . . . . . . . 45
Herbs with History . . . . . . . . . . . . . . . . 49

### Chapter Three: Flowering Plants

Ivy Geraniums (Pelargonium peltatum) . . . . . . . 54
Shy Cyclamen . . . . . . . . . . . . . . . . . . 57
Low-water Succulents. . . . . . . . . . . . . . . 60
Experiencing Euphorbia . . . . . . . . . . . . . . 64

Tending Roses in January. . . . . . . . . . . . . . . . . 67
Plant California Native Bulbs in Autumn. . . . . . . 70

## Chapter Four: Shrubs and Trees

Ceanothus Blue . . . . . . . . . . . . . . . . . . . . . 74
Zauschneria aka Epilobium . . . . . . . . . . . . . . 77
Spiny Barberries . . . . . . . . . . . . . . . . . . . . 80
Coyote Bush . . . . . . . . . . . . . . . . . . . . . . 83
Oleander: Toxic and Tough . . . . . . . . . . . . . . 86
Bamboo . . . . . . . . . . . . . . . . . . . . . . . . 89
Redwoods as Garden Plants . . . . . . . . . . . . . 92
Specimen Trees . . . . . . . . . . . . . . . . . . . . 95

## Chapter Five: Fruits of the Garden

Pomegranates . . . . . . . . . . . . . . . . . . . . . 99
Cultivating Fig Trees . . . . . . . . . . . . . . . . . 103
Growing and Preparing Table Olives . . . . . . . . 106
Jujube Dates . . . . . . . . . . . . . . . . . . . . . 109
Not-so-tropical Guava . . . . . . . . . . . . . . . . 112
Growing Grapes . . . . . . . . . . . . . . . . . . . 115
Mushrooms for the Garden . . . . . . . . . . . . . 118
Considering Food as Medicine . . . . . . . . . . . 121

## Chapter Six: Garden Design

Aromatic Entryways . . . . . . . . . . . . . . . . . 125
Green Roofs and Living Walls . . . . . . . . . . . 128
Apartment Gardening . . . . . . . . . . . . . . . . 132

~ Contents ~

Planting in Layers . . . . . . . . . . . . . . . . . . . . 136
Coral Reef Inspiration. . . . . . . . . . . . . . . . . 139
Tranquility in a Japanese Garden . . . . . . . . . 142
A Rooftop Container Garden in Greece . . . . . . . 145
Foiling Deer Gracefully . . . . . . . . . . . . . . . 148

CHAPTER SEVEN: LOW-WATER GARDENING

Microclimates in the Garden . . . . . . . . . . . . . 152
Drought-Tolerant Ferns . . . . . . . . . . . . . . . . 155
Gardening without Watering. . . . . . . . . . . . 159
Drought-Resistant Natives . . . . . . . . . . . . . 162
Planting Under Oaks . . . . . . . . . . . . . . . . . 165
Thriving in Clay Soil . . . . . . . . . . . . . . . . . 168

CHAPTER EIGHT: BACK TO BASICS

Weed Identification and Control . . . . . . . . . . . 172
Poisonous Garden Plants . . . . . . . . . . . . . . . 178
Rerouting Rain Runoff . . . . . . . . . . . . . . . . 184
Sowing Seeds . . . . . . . . . . . . . . . . . . . . . . 187
A Place for Invasives . . . . . . . . . . . . . . . . . 190
Dividing and Multiplying . . . . . . . . . . . . . . 194

**Index** . . . . . . . . . . . . . . . . . . . . . . . . . . . . 197

**About the Author** . . . . . . . . . . . . . . . . . . . 207

*To my daughters Laney and Piper,
who nourish gardens of their own.*

# *Introduction*

~

Since 1997, I have been gardening in a Mediterranean climate—first in Marin County, California, then in the southern Peloponnese of Greece. My garden in San Rafael overlooked San Pablo Bay. My garden above Vatika Bay, Greece, overlooks the Mediterranean itself.

I grew up in Colorado surrounded by plants. My father ran a garden store and plant nursery across the street from our house in Aurora, a suburb of Denver. When I was twelve, we moved north of Denver, where my father built greenhouses and grew carnations and roses commercially. He eventually had eleven acres under fiberglass. Our family's everyday conversations centered on the weather, the seasons, and their effects on plants.

When I moved to California, everything I knew about the seasons in Colorado became irrelevant. The Mediterranean climate of the San Francisco Bay area is almost the opposite of Colorado's. In Colorado, one plants only after May 31, to make sure plants will not freeze in a late snowfall. In Marin County, one plants in the fall, so new plants can benefit from the rainy winter season. I embarked on a long, slow learning curve.

Not long after I moved to San Rafael, California, I saw a notice in the local newspaper about how to become a Master Gardener. I was immediately intrigued and applied. The semester-long training course was fascinating and very thorough. Becoming a Master Gardener changed the way I thought about all aspects of gardening. I learned how to garden in the Mediterranean climate of my new home.

As a Master Gardener, one agrees to perform a certain number of hours of volunteer work each year. For my volunteer work, I chose to write articles for the Master Gardener column in the local newspaper, the Marin Independent Journal. This collection of essays compiles the articles I wrote for our Master Gardener column. I have revised and updated them.

In 2005, I began spending time in the southern Peloponnese. I bought a small olive farm and built a solar-powered house on it. Now I live on my olive farm. I had three raised beds built in the garden behind my house for herbs and flowers. My garden has several sections: an entryway garden, a garden on the terrace below my house, a rose garden below my bedroom balcony, and a garden that stretches beyond the raised beds. The olive trees that surround my house are an extended garden.

As I re-read and edited the essays for this book, I realized there are several threads that run through them:

I love plants and their background stories and various uses. As I learn about a plant, it becomes familiar to me. I treasure it in my garden as a friend.

I endeavor to create habitats that welcome birds, butterflies, bees and other pollinators. I do not use pesticides or herbicides, relying instead on organic solutions and hand-weeding.

My gardens are continuing works in progress. The essays in this book reflect not only the gardens I have created, but the dreams I have for my gardens. I write about my gardens as they are—and as I imagine them becoming.

I have become fascinated by Eastern and Western herbal medicine. The more I learn about the medicinal value of plants, the more medicinal plants I introduce in my garden.

*~ Introduction ~*

When I work in my garden, I am alone. But, for me, gardening is not a solitary pursuit. I happily find myself surrounded by other gardeners. We share information and seeds and plants. I treasure this communal aspect of gardening and the special bond that exists between people who nourish plants.

~
CHAPTER ONE
~

*Birds and Bees*

# *Blooms to Attract Hummingbirds*

~

John James Audubon called hummingbirds "glittering garments of the rainbow." These tiny, shimmering birds have always fascinated me. I wanted to see them in my own garden.

Most hummingbirds migrate from one location to another during the year, traveling hundreds, even thousands of miles. Once hummingbirds locate a garden that provides them with food, water, and cover for resting and potential nesting sites, they become loyal residents, returning year after year. Small as they are, they will aggressively defend their territory against larger birds and other trespassing hummingbirds.

As sources of food, hummingbirds are most interested in red flowers with tubular shapes to accommodate their long bills. They are also very efficient pollinators. As they probe deep into the flower for nectar, they pick up pollen on their crowns. The pollen is than transferred to the next flower they approach for food. Planting groupings of one species of flowers that hummingbirds like is beneficial to both birds and plants.

Native hummingbird plants and local hummingbird species have evolved together. The birds prefer reliable native sources of food that will provide for all their nutritional needs. Although cultivated plants such as impatiens have bright flowers, they are not necessarily good sources of the nectar hummingbirds require.

~ *Birds and Bees* ~

Using a selection of plants, I can provide for hummingbirds in my garden throughout the year. It is especially important to provide food for them during winter months when not much else is blooming. Flowering currants that bloom in mild climates in winter provide rich nectar for hummingbirds. *Ribes sanguineum* flowers in January and *Ribes malvaceum* blooms through winter into March. It is very important to choose the right species: *R. sanguineum* prefers a dry, sunny location, whereas *R. malvaceum* needs some water. Having planted *Ribes* species in my own garden, I can look forward to the annual return of the rufous hummingbird.

Coral bells (*Heuchera maxima*) is an early spring bloomer in my garden that attracts hummingbirds. Hundreds of tiny bell-shaped flowers hang from the wiry two-foot stems. The leaves of the plant form a compact mound and may be divided in the fall. *Heuchera maxima* is native to California's Channel Islands. In addition, there are a number of other species, such as *H. sanguinea*, native of Mexico and Arizona, that also appeal to hummingbirds.

Western columbine (*Aquilegia formosa*) blooms from the spring into the summer. It has scarlet or orange backward-projecting petals with contrasting yellow sepals and protruding stamens. The flowers nod gracefully on their stems. This species is native in a wide area from Utah to California to Alaska. It thrives in a woodland garden, prefers moist, rich soil and will tolerate filtered shade. In addition to nourishing hummingbirds, allowing columbines to go to seed will provide relished food for song sparrows, juncos and other small birds.

Several species of *Salvia* attract hummingbirds. They are drought tolerant, needing very little water in the summer. Blooming from spring through summer, *Salvia clevelandii* with its whorls of purplish flowers is an exception to the red, tube-shaped generalization. In my garden, I planted *S. clevelandii* for its spicy fragrance, which apparently makes little difference to hummingbirds. Like most birds, hummingbirds don't have much sense of smell. However, they are attracted to its nectar.

Its cousin, *Salvia greggii*, known as autumn sage, does have bright red tubular flowers, and is a notable hummingbird favorite in my garden. To promote flower production and to keep them from becoming too woody, salvia bushes should be cut back annually in the fall. I find this hard to do, but I have learned that it works.

Mexican sage (*S. leucantha*) also blooms in late summer. Its many stems produce vivid purple tubular flowers, which hummingbirds in my garden seem to love. It can be easily divided by digging up clumps of stems and replanting them.

For nectar-rich blooms in the fall, the California native fuchsia (*Zauschneria californica*, renamed *Epilobium*) is one hummingbirds cannot resist. In fact, one of its common names is Hummingbird Fuchsia. Its inch-long bright red or red-orange tubular flowers bloom at the end of arching stems. This drought-tolerant ground cover thrives in hot, dry summers and will spread by roots and reseeding. In my garden, I encourage its spreading, although *Zauschnerias* have been accused of becoming invasive.

Red-hot poker plants (*Kniphofia uvaria*), natives of South Africa, with their spikes of bright orange red flowers, quickly catch the attention of hummingbirds. This plant adds a vertical note to my garden plantings and is also easily divided.

Other plants that attract hummingbirds include monkey flower (*Mimulus aurantiacus*), firebird penstemon (*Pen-

*stemon gloxiniodes*), manzanita (*Arctostaphylos*), hummingbird fern (*Grevillea* 'Canberra') and island bush snapdragon (*Galvezia speciosa*).

By thoughtfully planting species of flowering plants that attract hummingbirds, I have created a welcoming habitat for these tiny jewels. They reciprocate by delighting me as they dart from bloom to bloom, glimmering in the sun.

# LuAnn's Garden

~

"My goal was to get rid of the lawn," LuAnn said. Her main objective was to reduce the amount of water her garden required—and maintaining a lawn in a region that is essentially a desert required way too much water. So Luann stripped down the front yard and put paths in it. Then she landscaped it with drought-tolerant plants.

She created a meadow-style garden, plants covering every inch of space, growing in seemingly natural profusion.

LuAnn chose more than two dozen different perennials to create a habitat garden requiring minimal water to maintain. To add color, she grew a few annuals, hollyhocks, cosmos, and Shasta daisies, from seed. In addition, LuAnn added a rose tree and nearly a dozen rose bushes. These needed more water than the rest of her garden. When she watered them occasionally by hand, she also gave an extra splash to the annuals.

To attract hummingbirds, LuAnn planted purple bush sage (*Salvia leucantha*) and autumn sage (*S. greggii*). She also planted four different *Penstemons*, montbretia (*Crocosmia crocosmiiflora*), California fuschia (*Zauschneria californica*, renamed *Epilobium*), several strawberry trees (*Arbutus unedo*), and rose-scented geraniums (*Pelargonium graveolens*).

Butterflies are attracted to the twelve-inch-high brick-red yarrow (*Achillea*) LuAnn used as a border. Nearby, she incorporated several different varieties of sedum whose fleshy leaves contrast with the feathery leaves of the yarrow. Butterflies are also attracted to the sea pink (*Armeria maritima*) LuAnn used as a ground cover under a pepper tree, the several different varieties of English and French lavender (*Lavandula*) she planted, and cosmos. Against the fence in the front yard, LuAnn placed a garden bench next to a group of lavender plants; when I sat amongst them, their fragrance washed over me.

Butterfly larvae (caterpillars) need food plants, and LuAnn's hollyhocks and roses provide a plentiful supply. It is important not to use any pesticides in a habitat garden since the pesticides kill all insects—including the insects one hopes to attract. LuAnn is happy to have some leaves with holes eaten by caterpillars in her garden, in the hopes that butterflies will soon emerge.

In the back yard, she preserved a strip of lawn but created a wide border of drought-tolerant habitat perennials. She also added a pond ringed with horsetails (*Equisetum hyemale*). "They may have been a mistake," LuAnn admits. Although she loves how natural they look next to the pond, they are extremely invasive and she has had to rigorously prune unwanted shoots. Next to the pond is a fig tree, heavily laden with fruit in early September. Her border includes a butterfly bush (*Buddleia*) and a rosemary bush pruned into a bonsai-like tree, both attractive to butterflies.

Other plants in the garden include Shasta daisies ("They reseed themselves and I pull some up like weeds," says LuAnn), society garlic, manzanita, and ground covers yerba Buena and snow-in-the-summer. Gaura plants flutter like their common name, butterflies-in-the-wind. There are two espaliered vines, a fall-blooming clematis and a purple potato vine. Wooly lambs ears (*Stachys*) provide silvery foliage that contrasts with the green leaves of penstemons and others.

LuAnn's watering schedule was once every third day for twenty minutes. Her drip system used half-gallon emitters. She relied on a generous layer of quarter-inch woodchips as mulch to keep the plants' roots from drying out. As it breaks down, the mulch adds organic matter to the soil. For fertilizer, LuAnn employed the castings of her active colony of worms.

Through her careful planning and thoughtful efforts, Luann created a magical space. Dozens of birds, butterflies and hummingbirds visit her garden regularly. The pond she installed melds seamlessly into the plants surrounding it. Luann's garden haven offers peace and nourishment to human visitors and wild creatures in equal measure.

# Sustainable Gardening

~

Sitting on the bench in my garden, I listen to four different birds' songs; I watch a hummingbird zip past, then pause to rest on the branch of a Monterey pine; I observe the full loads of pollen carried by our bees into their hives. White-and-black butterflies hover over garden blossoms. This wildlife and more thrives in our garden because I practice sustainable gardening.

Sustainable gardening is the popular umbrella term that covers gardening that conserves water, uses minimal (or no) chemicals, focuses on native plant species, and requires a minimum of maintenance by the gardener. It is a holistic approach to gardening that could also be termed self-sustaining because this type of garden does not require excessive input of water, plant material or human effort. Low-water, drought-tolerant, xeriscape, native, low-maintenance and habitat gardens all fall within the purview of sustainable gardening.

One aspect of sustainable gardening that particularly interests me is habitat gardening—that is gardening with a special awareness of providing food, water and cover for wildlife, as well as places animals may raise their young.

A sustainable garden that is wildlife-friendly includes:

- Food sources: Plants provide basic food for wildlife in the form of seeds, berries, nuts, fruits, nectar, sap, pollen, and foliage and twigs. Of course, in the garden ecosystem, some animals may become food for other animals, for example caterpillars or insects provide nourishment for birds.

- Water sources: Wildlife must have water to drink and in which to bathe. A water source in the garden may be a spring, a stream or a lake. For those of us without those natural resources, an artificial pond, a pump-driven fountain, a cement birdbath or even a depression in a stone can serve as a life-giving water source.

- Cover and protection: Wildlife need protection from predators and shelter and cover from the weather. Dense shrubs, brambles, evergreens, rock piles or walls, and wooded areas provide protection and shelter. A little messiness, in the form of piles of branches or untrimmed shrubs, around the edges of a garden can provide a refuge for birds and mammals.

- Places for young wildlife: To succeed as a habitat, a garden must provide a place for wildlife to bear and raise their young. Ideal locations are places predators have a hard time invading. These include mature trees, dead trees or snags, thickets or dense shrubs, wetlands and burrows. If your garden does not include any of these, home-made nesting boxes are an alternative. To create a habitat for butterflies, learn which plants are hosts for the larvae (caterpillars) of a given species and plant them in your garden. For example, milkweed is a host plant for larvae of the monarch butterfly; California Dutchman's pipe is a host plant for larvae of the pipevine swallowtail butterfly.

- Sustainable gardening practices: The way we manage the weeds, soil and water in our gardens affects the general habitat for wildlife living there. Chemicals from synthetic pesticides and fertilizers may be toxic to the insects and birds we are trying to encourage. Pulling weeds by hand is labor-intensive, but that labor can be minimized by heavy mulching, which will prevent the growth of weeds in the first place.

As an alternative to synthetic fertilizers, soil can be improved with organic fertilizer such as the sustainable aged manure produced by sheep or cows. Compost is a sustainable fertilizer because it is created from the waste plant material of the garden itself. Make compost tea by soaking compost in water, then use that water on thirsty plants.

Water in the garden should be managed to minimize waste. Xeriscape or water-wise landscaping will reduce the cost of irrigation, as will drip systems and soaker hoses. To reduce erosion of wildlife habitat, plant ground covers—preferably native species—or build terraces.

In my own garden, it has been easy to allow some messiness around the edges: places where I do not trim the bushes, others where unrestrained vines hide the neighbor's fence. These spots provide necessary cover and protection.

Fortunately, my garden is blessed with a number of mature trees. I have the previous owner to thank for his thoughtful plantings decades ago. Birds find refuge in the branches of pines and a redwood, a loquat tree and oaks.

As flowers turn to seeds, I leave them on the plants to feed the birds. Eventually, I prune back the plants and bushes, but I give the birds first priority.

For water sources, I chose artificial rocks molded to create pools where water naturally collects. They seemed less intrusive to me than traditional bird baths. I placed several among the garden beds. They are partially hidden—protected—by plants and maintain a natural appearance.

I only use organic fertilizer in my garden. I have convinced myself that weeding by hand is part of my personal fitness program. I have no desire to poison the birds and insects I am trying to so hard to attract to keep me company in my garden.

The birds reward me with their songs and fluttering wings. The insects hum. The bees make honey. Bright butterflies meander from flower to flower. Thanks to them, in my garden I find peace.

# How to Help Our Pollinators

~

Since 1950, the honey bee population in the United States has declined by 50 percent. The wild, or feral, honey bee population has declined by 70 percent. The general term for this phenomenon is colony collapse disorder. It is caused by a combination of factors including pesticides, parasitic mites, hybridization with aggressive strains of African bees, and loss of forage plants.

This may seem merely unfortunate until one considers some additional information:

- bees add eighteen billion dollars annually to the value of United States crops;
- one-third of the food supply of the United States depends on bee pollination, which makes the management and protection of pollinators an issue of paramount importance to the security of the United States food production system;
- honey bee colonies in more than twenty-three states have been affected by colony collapse disorder.

At the state level, a number of states have provided funds for research into colony collapse disorder that will lead to ways to reverse this trend and assist the rebuilding of healthy honey and native bee populations. States also have enacted laws to protect honey bees from pesticides. At the federal level, comprehensive legislation to protect honey bees has been proposed repeatedly, but never enacted.

Taking a small step to increase the number of honey bees in our community, last spring my husband and I purchased a bee box and a queen and a starter colony of about 4,000 bees. We had done some basic research ourselves and then discovered that a friend of ours had become an avid beekeeper. With our friend's help, we became beekeepers too. Placing the hive in the corner of our San Rafael garden, we soon observed the bees returning with their legs loaded with pollen. Over the summer, we managed the frames in the boxes, increasing the area the bees had to store their honey. We are now ready for our first honey harvest. Each generation of bees lives only about seven weeks, so our hive has already been home to several generations. Over the summer, our hive has grown considerably. The bees forage over a twelve square mile area, pollinating vegetables and flowers in gardens throughout our community. If keeping bees is of interest to you, I would highly recommend it.

If becoming a beekeeper is too much to contemplate, consider doing what you can to assist native bees. Native bees do not produce honey. But they are very active pollinators, responsible for pollinating nearly one-third of vegetable, fruit and nut crops, as well as almost all wildflowers. Rather than collecting pollen in sacs on their legs as honey bees do, native bees collect pollen on hairs on their stomachs. Thus, they prefer flat, open-faced flowers such as asters and Echinacea. They make their nests in the ground or in wood. Most live as solitary bees, in contrast to honey bees whose colonies number in the thousands. Whereas honey bees were introduced to North America from Europe, native bees originated here.

There are about 4,000 native bee species in North America, and 1,600 in California. Researcher have studied native bees in the Central Valley of California living in three types of habitat: they monitored native bee populations on organic farms close to wild habitat, organic farms distant from wild habitat, and conventional farms distant from wild habitat. They found that 80 percent of organic farms close to wild habitat could rely entirely on native pollinators, whereas only 50 percent of organic farms distant from wild habitat could do so. None of the conventional farms could rely on native pollinators alone. They determined that, overall, native bees provided 28 percent of pollination on conventional farms and 60 percent on organic farms. Increasing wild habitat is clearly important to supporting native bees that can serve as pollinators on farms. Farmers can leave strips of ground unplowed to allow bees to nest, and plant hedgerows of habitat plants to attract native bees.

Native bees have also suffered decimation in recent years. Their wild habitats of native plants have been replaced by farms and sprawling housing developments. Widespread pesticide use, on commercial farms and in domestic gardens, has killed many pests—and millions of native bees. But all is not lost: urban gardens can support native bees.

To support native bees, a variety of flowering plants is required. Not all bees like the same flowers, and bees require flowering plants throughout the season: spring, summer and fall. My garden already includes over a dozen plants native bees love: achillea, ceanothus, echium, erigeron, California poppy, lavender, penstemon, California coffeeberry, salvia, verbena, mint, nepeta, thyme, and rosemary.

Home gardeners can play a role in rebuilding the native bee population by planting the varieties of flowers on which native bees thrive—and bolster the health and productivity of our gardens at the same time. As I spent hours this spring and summer watching our new honey bees, I also became aware of the variety of native bees foraging from plant to plant. I felt proud to provide all these bees with a bountiful habitat—and equally humbled by their endless efforts and hard work to pollinate my garden and the food crops on which we rely, in the face of neglect and active decimation.

# *Beginning Beekeeping*

~

The honey bee population in the United States is declining. Articles have been written and news items aired lamenting this fact. Honey bees are indispensable unpaid agricultural workers: they are responsible for pollinating 90 percent of California's almond crop, for example. Although other insects also pollinate flowers, honey bees, living in large, exceedingly well-organized colonies, accomplish the most. Without pollinators, fruits, vegetables, nuts and other crops cannot develop.

In mid-April of 2007, my husband and I decided to take a small step to help maintain, and hopefully increase, the honey bee population in Marin County. This will, of course, benefit our own garden, as they pollinate our flowers and fruit trees. Since honey bees forage an area of about twelve square miles, our hive will also benefit our neighbors.

I asked a friend who keeps bees what I needed to do to get started. He told me to buy the book *Beekeeping for Dummies* by Howland Blackiston and read it. Then, he said, buy a bee hive. Once you set it up, you can buy your bees and install them.

That sounded simple. I bought the book, bought the hive—really a bottom, body, and top sold separately, and tried to find the bees. I called Bee Weavers in Texas, but they had sold out. The friendly woman I spoke with suggested I try to find bees locally. I found www.citybees.com, a website which provided a list of local suppliers and beekeeping organizations in the Bay Area. The nearest bee supplier was in Vacaville. I called and learned that April was the end of their season for selling bees: I could pick them up the next day, or wait until next year. Over the phone, I bought one "package" of bees. It would weigh three pounds, include about 4,000 bees and one small separate container with the queen inside.

My husband and I had read portions of our *Dummies* book. By this time, I had carefully painted the bee hive a very pale green to reflect heat and prolong the life of the wood. (Later I learned that some beekeepers prefer hives of unpainted wood. To eliminate unhealthy spores that can accumulate on the inside walls of the hive, they simply replace their hives every few years.) We would pick up our bees the next day. And we realized we desperately wanted someone to help us install them in their hive. I called the beekeepers I knew, but could not reach them. Then my husband called a friend in Sonoma County. Kathy responded enthusiastically. Not only would she come help us install the bees, she would bring a feeder, a screened bottom, a tin-covered top, sugar syrup to feed the new bees, and a stand to put our bee hive on. Our simple project assumed a new dimension.

Saturday morning, we drove to Vacaville. Tom, the supplier, went through a detailed description of how to install the bees and check on them and feed them for the first few weeks. Standing around his demonstration hive with several other bee purchasers, we realized we were entering a community. With admonitions to call him if we had any trouble or questions, Tom carried our package of bees to the car.

Although I had asked for Italian bees, Tom gave us Russian bees. Russian bees were imported to the United States fairly recently because they demonstrated resistance to a type of mite that can infect bees. The main advantage of

Italian bees is that they are better suited to Marin's Mediterranean climate. Both races of bees can thrive in Marin.

Kathy arrived soon after we got home. First we walked around the garden to find the right site for the hive. She selected a spot with good sun where the door to the hive would face east and where we could easily work behind it. She assembled a sturdy stand made of cinderblock pylons and four by fours.

Kathy and I put on our hats and veils. I put on long-sleeved leather gloves and gingerly carried the box of bees to the hive. Working bare-handed, Kathy sprayed some water on the bees to keep them from flying. Then she sharply tapped the box on the stand. The bees tumbled to the bottom of the box. Quickly, she pried the feed can out of the box. She slipped the plastic container holding the queen bee out of the box and I replaced the feed can to keep the other bees inside. Using rubber bands, Kathy fixed the queen's container onto one of the frames and put the frame back in the hive. Then Kathy sharply tapped the box down again, I removed the feed can, and, as I inverted the box, she tapped the bottom of the box so the bees fell through the open hole into the hive.

Carefully, she put the feeder on top of the hive. She poured sugar syrup into a shallow container with a cork float in it. She drizzled honey made by her own bees onto the wooden surfaces. Then I put the top on. The bees had reached their new home.

The next morning, as soon as the sun hit the hive, we watched bees busily leaving and returning. Our journey as beekeepers had just begun. We had much to learn. And we had discovered an active, generous, enthusiastic community of local beekeepers to help us along the way.

# *Backyard Beekeeping*

~

Our adventure in backyard beekeeping began in April, two and a half years ago.

My husband and I did some internet research, read *Beekeeping for Dummies* and, with the help of a beekeeping friend, installed one hive of bees in a corner of our garden. I had bought a wooden brood box, bottom, lid and frames to fill it.

Our friend Kathy brought us a stand for the hive of sturdy four-by-four planks and cinderblock pylons. The planks were six feet long. "Why so long?" we asked. "For your next two hives of bees," she replied.

At that point, we could not imagine having more than one hive of bees. We had purchased a box of about 4,000 bees and a queen from a supplier in Vallejo. Once Kathy had moved them into their new quarters, with my minimal help, she left.

My husband and I felt we had taken on responsibility for 4,000 new children. But the bees did not need our help. They began foraging the next day, hundreds of worker bees returning to the hive, sacs full of pollen on their legs.

We did not disturb the hive until the queen had time to begin laying eggs. Then, as new beekeepers, we disturbed our bees regularly. We had to see what was going on. Clad in sturdy white overalls, wearing veils and leather gloves, we opened the hive to check on the developing brood and honey production.

~ *Birds and Bees* ~

We added a queen excluder and honey super so the queen could not enter the upper box and the bees could fill the shallow frames with honey. They did so admirably.

In the fall, Dean oversaw our first honey extraction process. He rented an extractor from a local beekeepers' supply house and with another friend harvested pounds of honey from the hive.

Of course, he left sufficient stores for the bees to eat during the winter months. We gave gifts of honey to our neighbors and they responded with gifts of applesauce and persimmon bars from trees that had flourished exceptionally well since bees had moved onto our block.

In the spring, it appeared at first that all was well. The hive had made it through the winter. Then, all at once, the bees were gone. Had our hive suffered what is known as colony collapse? Had they become infected with disease? What could have happened? We could not answer the question, and an inspection of the empty hive offered no clues.

But it did not occur to us to give up keeping bees. Our garden was thriving, thanks to the increased pollination contributed by our bees. Our neighbors' gardens were thriving, too. We enjoyed sitting in the garden watching the bees and silently communicating with them. We thoroughly enjoyed eating the honey our bees produced and giving jars of it away. Our second spring of beekeeping, we replenished our hive with new bees. And we bought a second hive and filled it, too.

This spring, again one hive collapsed or disappeared, so we split the remaining, healthy hive to replace the bees in the hive that failed.

The healthy older hive was so prolific that before spring had turned to summer, we bought a third hive box, split the hive again, and, as Kathy had predicted, filled the hive base to capacity.

Beekeeping has added a new dimension our garden and to our lives. My husband and I entered a new community—the community of beekeepers—the moment we purchased our first box of bees. We inspired a friend to keep bees herself. As a result, our friendship deepened. Together, she and I extracted honey from both our hives in her basement workroom—a messy but deeply satisfying job. Relations with our neighbors improved as we proffered gifts of honey. Becoming a beekeeper has brought me unexpected joy.

~

CHAPTER TWO

~

*Flowering Herbs*

# Rosemary Means Remembrance

~

*"There's rosemary, that's for remembrance;
pray, love, remember."*

—William Shakespeare, Hamlet, Act 4, Scene 5

For centuries, rosemary (*Rosmarinus officinalis*) has been appreciated as a symbolic, medicinal and culinary herb. A native of the Mediterranean region, rosemary thrives in a range of climates.

Rosemary is a shrub with needle-like leaves and tiny blue flowers that bloom in spring and fall. It is one of the first plants to flower in my garden and different varieties range in color from medium blue to white. It is known for attracting adult butterflies. Bees use the nectar to produce flavorful honey.

Rosemary thrives in tough growing conditions. It can tolerate hot sun and ocean spray. It is drought-tolerant once established and can withstand windy conditions. Its roots create a dense network that controls erosion on hillsides.

In my garden, rosemary is particularly valuable because the deer do not eat its sharp, stiff leaves. Different varieties perform different functions on our hillside. In one area, I planted *R. officinalis* 'Prostratus' which spreads lavishly across the ground. It is a low shrub and serves as an effective ground cover. Its branches twist and turn back upon themselves, creating interesting shapes and forms.

~ *Flowering Herbs* ~

Near the fence, I planted *R. officinalis* 'Tuscan Blue.' This is an upright shrub and is developing into an attractive hedge. Originally, I had planted one of them near a walkway, an inappropriate spot. After a year or so, it grew too tall and I decided to transplant it. Because of their extensive root systems, rosemary plants are not generally good candidates for transplanting. I nearly killed this one. However, even though about half of the plant died, within a couple of years, it managed to return to vigorous growth—a testimony to its tough character.

Above a low wall, I planted several *R. officinalis* 'Huntington Carpet.' This is a cultivar of the 'Prostatus' variety. It has deep-blue flowers and will eventually drape down over the wall. This newly-landscaped area is under a venerable oak tree. Rosemary, because of its low water requirements, is suitable for planting under oaks. However, again I may have made a mistake. Beneath the wall is a graveled landing with French café table and chairs. My intention is to enjoy lunch in the shade of the oak. I have already noticed that when the rosemary is blooming, insects that were initially attracted to the blossoms are equally attracted to my sandwich.

Being able to propagate plants in my garden gives me special pleasure. Rosemary is an especially good candidate. It can be propagated either by stem cuttings or layering. For stem cutting, take a four- to five-inch sprig of healthy new growth from the top of the plant and root it in moist sand. It will be ready for planting in soil in approximately six weeks. To layer, use a wire staple to peg a branch to the ground and mound soil over it. This is best done in fall or winter when the rains will promote new root growth. By summer, the new plant can be clipped from the mother plant and carefully moved.

There are many uses for fresh rosemary. As a culinary herb, it can be chopped and added to butter for a savory accompaniment to rolls. If one is more ambitious and baking, the chopped herb can be added to bread dough, one tablespoon to each loaf. It can be added to fruit salads to enhance sweetness. I sprinkle it over new potatoes when I roast them in the oven. Rosemary leaves are typically added to pork and lamb dishes. When grilling salmon, I place a branch of rosemary on a sheet of foil under the fish.

Springs of rosemary can be added to hot bathwater which releases the leaves' essential oil. Its leaves may also be used to brew a tea reputed by herbalists to serve as a tonic, astringent, and to alleviate headaches.

Because it keeps its leaves year-round, rosemary is a symbol of fidelity and remembrance. It is used in bridal wreathes and bouquets for its symbolic value as well as its beauty. At funerals, mourners toss sprigs into the grave to signify they will not forget their loved one.

# Long-lasting Lavender

~

The Spanish lavender (*Lavendula stoechas*) in my garden is just beginning to bloom. It seems a bit early this year. In fact, it may be blooming before the yellow narcissus have finished. If so, the contrast will be magnificent. Of the four species of lavender I have planted, Spanish lavender blooms first. Its flowers are dark purple, each one topped with a whirligig of intensely colored bracts. I planted a large clump of seven plants, expecting each one to grow to three feet across. So far, only two of the seven have grown that large. However, California poppies have seeded themselves in between the lavender plants. I am looking forward to a bright show in a few weeks time.

Lavenders are native to the Mediterranean countries, with climates characterized by dry summers and wet winters, and moderate temperatures year-round. However, lavenders are not limited to Mediterranean climates and some varieties can survive winter snows.

Lavenders do not require much summer water, making them perfect candidates for low-water-use gardens. They do require watering the first year, but once plants are established, over-watering may kill them. Although several sources maintain that lavenders need loose, fast-draining soil, I have observed that they are growing very well in the dense clay soil of my garden. If soil is too rich, the plants will develop lovely foliage, but few flowers. The Spanish lavender in my upper garden is the champion self-seeder among my garden plants.

All my lavenders benefit from pruning after they bloom. It is safe to cut off as much as one-third of the plant. Pruning more than that is too stressful and may weaken the plant. When I don't cut my lavenders back, the old stems become woody, old foliage turns black and only the new growth on stem tips is green. After three or four years, the bushes (they will have become bushes in that time!) may become scraggly. Don't be afraid to replace them. In my garden, I have combined lavender with rosemary, santolina, nepeta, yarrow and verbena, which all require similar amounts of water, soil and sun.

Lavender's name comes from the Latin *lavare*, meaning to wash. Because of its fresh fragrance, in Roman times lavender was used in soap, and sprigs may have been added to the wash water itself. After the fall of the Roman Empire, bathing went out of fashion. In Elizabethan times, lavender perfumes were used to cloak unpleasant odors.

In cooking, lavender leaves and flowers are used in savory dishes to flavor meats and sauces. According to herbalist Jethro Kloss, lavender flowers can be steeped in boiling water as a tonic tea which prevents fainting and allays nausea. I have a favorite recipe for lavender lemonade which calls for infusing fresh or dried lavender blooms: combine one cup of sugar with two and one-half cups of water and bring to a boil over medium heat, stirring to dissolve the sugar. Add a generous handful (about one-quarter cup) fresh lavender blooms or one tablespoon dried lavender blooms (no stems) to the sugar water, cover, and remove from heat. After it stands from twenty minutes up to several hours, strain the mixture. Add one cup of freshly squeezed lemon juice and another two and a half cups of water. Stir well and serve over ice, garnished with fresh lavender sprigs.

*~ Flowering Herbs ~*

In my garden, in addition to Spanish lavender, I have planted English lavender (*L. angustifolia*). According to one source, it is the most widely planted lavender and is the classic lavender used for perfumes and sachets. I planted the dwarf variety 'Hidcote' which grows in a compact one-foot dome, then sends out long two-foot spikes with flowers at the tip. These long spikes are essential if one is making lavender wands. These pretty gifts require twenty or so spikes, a few yards of quarter-inch ribbon and a little practice to make. With the ribbon, tie the spikes together just underneath the flowers, then turn the cluster upside down. Fold back the stems and use the ribbon to weave a tight enclosure around the hidden flower heads.

I have also planted French lavender (*L. dentata*) with its distinctive tooth-edged leaves. It blooms profusely with clusters of pale purple flowers on short stems. During a past mild winter, it bloomed almost continually.

The fourth variety of lavender in my garden is a variety of *L. intermedia* called 'Provence,' grown in France commercially for use in perfume. For hundreds of years, the valleys of Provence have been filled with the color and distinctive fragrance of this lavender.

For use in sachets, I cut and dry the spent blooms of 'Provence,' French and English lavender. I have read that the correct procedure is to cut flowers from their stems just as the color begins to show, but I am unwilling to sacrifice their color and fragrance in the garden. By contrast, I have determined that the fragrance of Spanish lavender is weak and the blooms are not worth the effort to gather and dry.

I am trying to improve the overall habitat in my garden for beneficial insects and birds. My lavender plants are important in that regard. They provide nectar for bees and other insects from spring, when the Spanish lavender blooms, through English lavender in the summer and fall when 'Provence' is at its best. And if we have a mild winter, the French lavender keeps providing insect food year-round.

# *Achilleas: Legends and Lore*

~

My first acquaintance with *Achilleas* was made in the Rocky Mountains. Growing alongside every trail was a wildflower with flattish white clusters of flowers and feathery gray-green leaves. It was yarrow, officially *Achillea millefolium*. I became fascinated by its many uses and the legends and lore surrounding it. Over the years, it has become a staple in my garden in Marin.

Yarrow is called *Achillea* because, according to legend, Achilles used the bruised raw fresh herb to staunch the blood of his warriors' wounds. Unfortunately, its healing properties could not save Achilles himself. That yarrow actually does have value in healing wounds is reflected in its many common names: 'soldier's woundwort', 'knight's millefollium', 'herbe militaris', 'bloodwort', and 'staunchweed.' Millefolium, meaning "thousand leaves," refers to yarrow's double-divided lacy leaves that look like little feathers.

In my garden I prefer to grow native California plants, and some *Achilleas* meet that criterion. In fact, *Achilleas* are native to many parts of the world. *A. ageratifolia*, with its low mat of silvery leaves, is otherwise known as Greek yarrow and is native to the Balkan region. *A. taygetea*, a favorite for its dense clusters of bright yellow flowers, is native to the Levant, the eastern Mediterranean region which stretches across north Africa to the Middle East. *A. millefolium* or common yarrow is listed by several sources as a California native. However, it appears to be very widely spread across the United States, Canada, and Europe, and can claim native status in a number of locations.

Many colors of *Achilleas* have been developed as cultivars and hybrids. Of the six varieties of *Achillea* I have planted, 'Coronation Gold' is my favorite. At the entrance of my garden path, its bright yellow blossoms on three-foot stems serve as welcoming candles.

Further down the path are pale yellow 'Moonshine' and 'Salmon Beauty' with pinkish blossoms. 'Paprika' has brick-red flowers. These varieties are later blooming than 'Coronation Gold,' are about two feet tall and have relatively weaker stems.

Recently I planted *A. wilzeckii*, a short plant, less than twelve inches tall, with white flowers. In contrast to the tiny individual flowers in the flat-topped clusters typical of *Achilleas*, this one's individual flowers are much larger and each daisy-like blossom in the flat umbel is easily distinguished. The pure white flowers with yellow centers provide effective contrast in a low border mixed with the electric-blue flowers of perennial lobelia. The leaves of *A. wilzeckii* are dentate (tooth-like) rather than feathery and the plant grows in a low mound.

The final variety of *Achillea* in my garden is *A. borealis*, a pink yarrow from California's Channel Islands. In just a few weeks, the plants have grown from four inches tall in four-inch pots to fifteen-inch plants about to bloom. They have light green foliage in contrast to the grayish foliage of my other *Achilleas*.

Propagating plants in my garden always gives me great pleasure. When clumps of *Achillea* become crowded, they can and should be divided, thus providing a source of new plants. I have also observed that 'Coronation Gold' produces baby plants on its stems. If those stems are pinned to

~ *Flowering Herbs* ~

the ground with a wire hoop, the tiny plants will take root and grow. They can also be removed from the mother plant and rooted in potting soil. 'Moonshine,' 'Salmon Beauty,' and 'Paprika' behave differently. After blooming, the central plant dies down and a group of tiny plants appears the next season in a ring around the edge of the previous plant. These tiny sprouts will flourish if watered regularly, developing into a cluster of flowering plants. This self-propagating aspect of *Achilleas* is one reason I like them so much. I generally deadhead, that is, remove dead flowers, regularly, so my *Achilleas* do not have a chance to produce seed.

*Achillea* seed is available and, according to several sources, *Achilleas* may be employed as a lawn substitute. One can prepare the site as for a lawn, broadcast yarrow seeds in the spring, water, and eventually mow the plants several times a year. Once established, *Achilleas* are very drought tolerant, so these low-growing feathery leaves could produce a pleasing substitute for water-guzzling grass.

*Achillea* flowers are excellent for use in both fresh and dried flower arrangements. In order to preserve their color, dry the flowers in silica gel.

*Achilleas* have also made their way into the realm of philosophy. For centuries, the strong, straight stalks of yarrow have been dried and used by Chinese philosophers for throwing the *I Ching*.

To use *Achilleas* for their medicinal properties in infusions, they should be gathered while in bloom and dried in a warm room. According to tradition, an infusion of *Achillea*, made by pouring one pint of boiling water over one ounce of the dried herb, may be used as a regular hair wash to prevent baldness.

*Achillea* features in one memorable event in my family's lore. My parents and I were camping in the Colorado Rockies when my father developed an excruciating toothache. We were many miles from a dentist. It would be a full day before we could get to one. My father packed a wad of yarrow leaves around his tooth. It stopped hurting. Not only that, the effect lasted twenty-four hours.

One final use of yarrow I find particularly charming. This is taken from *Stalking the Healthful Herbs* by Euell Gibbons:

"Sew an ounce of the herb into a little flannel square and place it under your pillow. Before going to bed, recite,

'Thou pretty herb of Venus' tree,
Thy true name is yarrow.

Now who my bosom friend must be,
Pray tell thou me tomorrow.'

If all has been properly done, just before you awaken the next morning, you will see your future husband or wife in a vision."

# *Superlative Salvias*

~

Growing up near Denver, Colorado, I knew salvia only as the bright red spikes of annuals in municipal flowerbeds. It wasn't until many years later that I learned the number and variety of plants the genus *Salvia* includes! Salvias belong to the mint family Lamiaceae. Their leaves are delightfully pungent and many are ornamental as well.

*Salvia splendens*, of my childhood memories, was introduced to Europe around 1800 by Baron Alexander von Humboldt, the German aristocrat who sent home many plants from his travels in South America. A perennial in its native Brazil and Mexico, it is often grown as an annual further north. Some gardeners find its scarlet too gaudy, whereas hummingbirds love it.

Another common salvia, *S. offinalis*, has been appreciated as a medicinal herb for centuries. A European native, its name derives from the Latin word *salvus*, meaning healed or saved, and *officinalis*, meaning it was on the official list of medicinal herbs. In this context, during the Middle Ages it was reputed to have marvelous healing powers, effective against fevers, sore throats, typhoid fever, headaches, flatulence and many other complaints. Its common name is sage and no herb garden was without it.

Today, *S. offinalis* is better known as a culinary herb, although this use may have originally stemmed from its medicinal properties. According to one source, sage was first added to stuffing for turkeys, sausages and pork dressing to counteract the indigestion that may be caused by these rich, greasy foods. Though we may have forgotten the original purpose, we like the taste. Sage is a welcome addition not only to meat dishes, but also to leafy salads. Its fresh, green leaves can be brewed into a soothing tea. The Chinese are reported to have valued sage tea so highly that they would trade many pounds of their own tea for one pound of sage. Other salvias used as seasoning for food include Cleveland's sage (*S. clevelandii*) and pineapple sage (*S. elegans*), recommended for use in cool drinks and fruit salads.

Salvias are widespread. Over sixty species of Salvia grow in the United States. They range from creeping ground covers (*S. sonomensis*) to bushes seven feet tall (*S. uliginosa*). Flower colors range from white to red to purple and shades in-between. Many are popular because they are drought-tolerant and deer-resistant. The salvias in my California garden thrive in clay soil, a definite plus. However, perennial salvias' root areas are sensitive to cold temperatures and should be well mulched before winter. If you decide to grow salvias from seeds, expect that they will germinate slowly, taking two to three weeks. One source suggests that some salvias' roots may be lifted in the fall and stored in moist sand over winter. The new start from roots is reportedly more magnificent than from seeds.

One of the most frequently seen salvias in the San Francisco Bay area is Mexican bush sage (*S. leucantha*). It grows to three or four feet with graceful, arching stems of velvety purple spikes. In the fall, some say old stems should be cut to the ground. New shoots will emerge in the spring and a single plant will evolve into a colony. In my experience, drastic pruning has been very stressful to the plants and some have taken a full season to recover. Mexican sage transplants well and I have dug up and replanted several sections of a colony, a very effective form of propagation.

~ *Flowering Herbs* ~

Autumn sage is also a three- to four-foot bush. I bought one and was so pleased with its small green leaves and bright red flowers that seemed to go on blooming forever, I bought two more. I didn't realize that there are many colors of *S. greggii*—these two had magenta flowers and the bushes grew into altogether different shapes.

Creeping sage (*S. sonomensis*), as its name implies, is a low-growing ground cover. Its flower stems reach upward with violet blossoms in a spike of whorls. Creeping sage thrives on dry slopes in chaparral and woodlands. It roots frequently along its stems. It may be too invasive for some gardens, but as a fast-growing, drought-tolerant ground cover, in some situations it may be useful. I plan to try it on a south-facing, lightly-shaded slope, hoping it will spread.

Hummingbird sage (*S. spathacea*) grows two- to three-feet tall from creeping rhizomes. The purplish red tubular flowers appear in whorls and are very attractive to hummingbirds. It grows easily from seed and volunteers may proliferate. A large, coarse plant, it may be used among other large perennials or in a background planting.

Cleveland's sage (*S. clevelandii*), also called fragrant sage, is a rounded three-foot shrub which grows wild on dry slopes. On a warm day, its fragrance floats beyond it on the breeze. I first encountered it by Muir Beach and immediately bought some for my garden. Whenever I walk by one, I pick a leaf for the pleasure of crushing it for its perfume.

Another California native, black sage (*S. mellifera*) has been variously described. Glenn Keator, in *Native Shrubs of California*, called it "perhaps the least attractive [sage]," however, "excellent for bees." Judith Lowry, in *Gardening with a Wild Heart*, suggests using black sage as a "keynote plant, to be repeated throughout the garden, [to] give a garden 'bones,' a structure that they can follow throughout.

From annual bedding plants to kitchen herbs to the bones of a garden, salvias are most versatile and useful. In my garden, they add color, fragrance, tasty leaves for cooking, and structure: superlative salvias, indeed.

# *Lemon Verbena*

~

A friend of mine is planting a small garden bed outside her front door. To welcome her guests and to provide herbs for use in cooking, she has decided to plant some aromatic herbs there. Rosemary and lavender topped the list for their welcoming fragrances. Then she chose oregano, for frequent use in all kinds of dishes. The fourth plant she chose is another one I know from my own garden, lemon verbena.

Lemon verbena, *Aloysia triphylla*, is a native of South America, widespread from Chile to Argentina to Peru. It was brought to Europe by the Spanish in the 1700s and introduced into England in 1784. Its botanical name *Aloysia* is in honor of Maria Luisa de Parma (1751-1819), wife of King Carlos IV of Spain. In several languages, including Spanish, Slovak, Greek, and Hebrew, Louisa is its common name. The species name, *triphylla*, refers to the manner in which three (*tri*) leaves (*phyla*) grow from a common node. Verbena, its common name, derives from a Latin word meaning "leafy branch."

In Latin America, it is a small tree that grows as tall as fifteen feet. Even on the Isle of Wight and in other sheltered localities in England, it is reputed to reach that height. Other sources refer to it as a one to three meter high deciduous plant. That is more consistent with my experience: the lemon verbena in my garden is a leggy three-foot shrub. Its thin stems sprout narrow green leaves and its blooms are small white flowers on terminal panicles. But although it is not an especially prepossessing plant, it is one of my favorites.

Every time I pass it, I crush a leaf for its light, fresh fragrance. The fragrance and flavor of the leaves make it useful for tea and flavoring various dishes. Its leaves are also used medicinally.

As a traditional herbal remedy, lemon verbena is used as an infusion to relieve digestive track spasms, strengthen the nervous system, and to reduce fevers. It is used to reduce stress, and acts as a sedative. In Chinese medicine, it is used to treat menstrual disorders. To make an infusion, pour a cup of boiling water over one-quarter cup of fresh leaves, or two teaspoons of dried leaves, let stand for five minutes, and strain it before drinking. The infusion is also delicious as iced tea in summer.

The dried leaves of lemon verbena are known for retaining their fragrance for years -- excellent ingredients in potpourri. *The Kitchen and Herb Gardener* by Richard Bird and Jessica Houdret includes a recipe for potpourri that uses two cups of lemon verbena leaves mixed with one cup of chamomile flowers, one cup of dried calendula petals, a stick of cinnamon, the dried peel of one lemon and one teaspoon of orris root powder. Two or three drops of lemon verbena essential oil may be added to the initial mixture, or to refresh it from time to time.

Lemon verbena leaves are tough, so to use them in cooking they must either be finely chopped or removed before serving. A few leaves may be put in the bottom of a buttered cake pan before the batter is spooned in. When the cake is baking, the leaves will release their oil and impart a lemony flavor. When the cake is cooling upside down on the rack, remove the leaves. Alternatively, the leaves may be finely chopped and added to cake batter or to scones. Chopped leaves may be added to fruit salads or to fruit sorbet. They

*~ Flowering Herbs ~*

may also be used to flavor fish soup and stews and are good with poultry.

Commercial applications for the essential oil are in perfumery, especially in making toilet water and eau de cologne. It is used in fine soap—in French soap, verbena is *verveine*. If you can't find the scented soap, fresh leaves may be added to a hot bath to relieve achy muscles.

Lemon verbena likes sun—preferable six hours a day or more. Although some sources say it requires a light loam soil and plenty of water, at least one source suggests a traditional herb soil on the dry side. My own lemon verbena grows in clay soil and receives little extra water in the dry summer months. Our winter rains are sufficient to keep it growing. It does not tolerate frost and in cold climates should be brought indoors in winter.

Lemon verbena is semi-deciduous, so don't worry when it loses its leaves. They will grow again in spring. Trim it in early summer, and make cuttings from the excess vegetation. Remove dead stems in early summer and prune regularly during the year. Plants may be divided from late fall to early spring. A minimum of care and attention will provide plentiful fragrant leaves to enjoy year-round.

# It's About Thyme

~

In my garden, I imagined steps covered in low green plants that would be soft underfoot, but that could withstand ordinary traffic; plants that would release a pleasing aroma to welcome visitors. And so I made the acquaintance of woolly thyme. I bought a flat of *Thymus lanuginosus* and planted two-inch square sections about six inches apart. It soon covered the steps and began spilling down the bank. Only about three inches high, it glows with pale pink flowers in the spring. It appreciates some summer water, but not too much: in an area next to a patch of sword ferns, it died, apparently from excessive dampness.

Woolly thyme is not the only thyme in my garden. Varieties of thyme have been used in cooking and for medicinal and symbolic purposes for thousands of years.

On my kitchen deck, I have a pot of lemon thyme. It is a compact shrub about twelve inches high; the tiny leaves have yellow borders. Of the several varieties of thyme used in cooking, lemon thyme (*T. citriodoris*) is my favorite. Its light citrus tang pairs perfectly with fish and vegetable dishes. Other varieties used in cooking are common thyme (*T. vulgaris*) and creeping thyme (*T. serpyllum*). One caraway-flavored variety was traditionally used to rub baron of beef before it was roasted. It was known as Herbe Baronne, reflected in its Latin name, *T. herba-barona*.

Thyme grows wild in southern France. There, because of its easy availability and exceptional flavor, it is one of the primary components of *bouquet garni*. Along with pars-

*~ Flowering Herbs ~*

ley sprigs and bay leaves, it is used to flavor sauces, soups and stews. The whole herb is used, either fresh or dried. Thyme is an essential part of the aromatic blend known as Herbes de Provence. Lavender is also one of the Herbes de Provence and according to René Gattefossé, the French father of aromatherapy, thyme is a "faithful companion of lavender. It lives with it in perfect harmony and partakes alike of its good and its bad fortune."

Wild thyme covers the dry, rock-strewn hillsides of Greece. The warm sun releases its volatile oils and its scent is carried on summer breezes. Thyme honey is abundant and highly prized. In *The Book of Herb Lore,* Lady Rosalind Northcote said that among the Greeks, thyme denoted graceful elegance, and the phrase "to smell of thyme" was an expression of praise for those with admirable style.

Thymol is the phenol that is thyme's "active ingredient." Thymol has been used as an antiseptic since ancient times: the Sumerians recorded using it in 3000 B.C.E. The Egyptians used it for embalming. According to Mrs. M. Grieve's 1931 treatise *A Modern Herbal,* "The antiseptic properties of Thyme were fully recognized in classic times, there being a reference in Virgil's *Georgics* to its use as a fumigator, and Pliny tells us that, when burnt, it puts to flight all venomous creatures."

In the mid-1600s, the English herbalist Nicholas Culpeper wrote in *The Complete Herbal,* "It is a noble strengthener of the lungs, as notable a one as grows....It purges the body of phlegm, and is an excellent remedy for shortness of breath." Thyme reputedly relieves chest congestion in three ways: first, it stimulates the movement of mucus out of the chest cavity; second, it provides antimicrobial chemicals to ensure that the infection is killed; and third, it acts as an antispasmodic, which helps with the pain associated with coughing. Commercially, thymol is used in over-the-counter cough syrups and cold remedies. To make your own cough-relieving tea, add two tablespoons of dried thyme to one cup boiling water, let stand ten minutes, then strain and drink.

The word thyme probably evolved from the Greek word *thymon*, which means courage. Greeks used it in their baths and as incense in their temples. The Romans bathed in thyme-scented waters to give them courage in battle. The Romans may be responsible for spreading thyme throughout Europe. In the Middle Ages, as a token of courage, women would embroider a sprig of thyme leaves onto their knights' tunics.

There are over three hundred varieties of thyme and many are available as seed. Or you may buy it as a bedding plant at your local nursery, as I did. Existing clumps may be successfully divided, as long as each section has some roots attached. Thyme prefers lots of sun and dry, sandy soil. Heavy mulch will protect the plants from severe cold. Once established, plants need little care, however, they should be pruned to remove dead flowers and old woody stems. Feed annually with compost or compost tea, as thyme tends to deplete the soil.

Thyme now grows wild from the Scottish Highlands to the shores of the Mediterranean—and has proven be a perfect plant for my garden.

# Chinese Garden Herbs

~

Recently I visited the University of California's Botanical Garden, located on the hill above the main Berkeley campus, and found myself in a section of the garden devoted to Chinese medicinal herbs.

While many of the plants were new to me, I saw a number of familiar plants—even some I grow in my own garden. I may never use these plants to prepare an herbal tea or tincture, but knowing more about their medicinal value increases my interest in them and enriches the time I spend in the garden.

Chinese medicine includes two concepts of *qi* (pronounced "chee"): bad *qi*, or pathogenic factors (*fan zhi*) and good *qi*, or beneficial factors (*zheng zhi*). The fundamental principle is that pathogenic factors should be eliminated from the system and beneficial factors should be built up.

For a first look at Chinese medicinal herbs we may find in our own gardens, let us consider some that help the body eliminate bad *qi*. These include herbs that promote sweating, diuretics, laxatives and expectorants. In each of these categories, we find plants that we know.

Herbs to promote sweating include the following:

- Peppermint leaf (*Mentha piperita*) is used to promote sweating and reduce fever, resolve phlegm and open the sinuses. It is also used to stimulate digestion, settle the stomach and reduce stagnation of liver *qi*. Peppermint leaf may be used as an infusion, for inhalation or in the form of an essential oil.

- Catnip herb (*Nepeta*) is used to promote sweating, circulate the *qi* and promote rest. It may be sipped hot as an herbal infusion. In my garden, I value it for its soft, gray-green foliage and lavender flowers. Knowing its benefits, I may try it for tea.

Herbs to use as diuretics include:

- Goldenrod (*Solidago*) is used to promote urination, drain fluid congestion and promote tissue repair. It is used as an infusion and may be used as a wash to reduce infection. Plants grow best in not-too-rich soil, which would recommend it for my garden.

- Dandelion leaf (*Taraxacum officinale*) is a powerful diuretic. This is one plant that is more plentiful in my garden than I would wish. The young leaves are reputed to have a detoxifying effect when eaten in salads in spring.

Herbs that can be used as laxatives include:

- Senna leaf (*Senna acutifolia* or *S. angustifolia*) is used to promote bowel movement, stop bleeding and reduce infection. It may be used as a tincture or infusion, or chopped up, soaked, then strained. This is a very powerful herbal remedy; use it for a very short time only.

~ *Flowering Herbs* ~

Senna is also known as Cassia, and there are many species of these trees and shrubs covered with bright yellow flowers that thrive in California.

- Aloe resin (*Aloe vera*) is used to promote bowel movement, stimulate digestion and counter *qi* stagnation. It may also be used to soothe the stomach in cases when ulcers are threatened or present. Aloe resin is a powdered concentrate derived from the juice of aloe leaves. A tincture of the leaves is also used. In the West, we are more familiar with the use of the juice of aloe leaves as an effective remedy for burns.

Plants that may be used as expectorants include:

- Thyme (*Thymus vulgaris*) is used to promote expectoration, resolve viscous phlegm, relieve coughing and circulate lung *qi*. Thyme herb is used as a daily restorative. Its strongest form is as an essential oil; the tincture may be used daily. I grow three species of thyme in my garden. I will probably never bother to crush those tiny leaves and steep them in alcohol to create a tincture, but it pleases me to know how useful thyme may be.

- Basil (*Ocimum basilicum*) is used to promote expectoration, open the chest and sinuses, and stimulate digestion. An infusion of the herb is weak; the essential oil or tincture brings out basil's full potential. Inhalations using the essential may be used for decongesting the sinuses in head colds.

These plants have been used for thousands of years in Chinese traditional medicine. The more I learn about these plants, the more I appreciate their beauty and versatility—and the more privileged I feel to spend time among them in my garden every day.

# Herbs with History

~

Chateaudun, in northcentral France, boasts a historical herb garden. The medieval chateau dates from the twelfth century. In the fifteenth century, it was home to Jean de Dunois, comrade-in-arms of Joan of Arc.

The medicinal herb garden lies to the side of the central courtyard, in the shadow of the tall, circular tower called the donjon. Its square plots are edged in neatly trimmed boxwood. Inside the perimeter of each plot, a number of herbs grow in less orderly profusion.

I was intrigued to recognize a number of species that flourish in my own garden in Marin. It struck me that a thread of continuity runs between the ancient fortress of Chateaudun, at the edge of its steep embankment in France, and my hillside garden overlooking San Pablo Bay. Rosemary, lavender, Achillea, oregano, valerian, mint, basil, thyme, lemon, bay and aloe grow in both gardens. Other Mediterranean herbs I was familiar with also grow at Chateaudun: anise, borage, chamomile, tarragon, sorrel, sage, lovage and lemon balm.

Since I have written about the herbs that grow in my garden before, I will focus on the other herbs grown in the medieval garden. In general, Mediterranean herbs prefer full sun, can be grown in poor soil and should not be overwatered.

- Anise (*Pimpinella anisum*) is an annual whose first growth is a clump of bright green roundish leaves. A stem with feathery leaves shoots up from the clump.

Clusters of white flowers appear at stem tips in summer. After about four months, licorice-flavored seeds will be ready to harvest. The feathery leaves can be used in salads and the seeds in baked goods. Medicinally, the seeds were used to aid digestion and sweeten bad breath.

- Borage (*Borago officinalis*) is an annual that provides good drought-tolerant groundcover. Its bristly leaves have a cucumber flavor: Use small tender leaves in salads or steam larger leaves as greens. Its star-shaped blue flowers can be used as an edible garnish. Medicinally, leaves were supposed to relieve melancholy. Also reputed to bring courage, borage was added to the final stirrup cup of those departing to fight in the Crusades.

- Chamomile (*Matricaria recutita*) is an annual with daisy-like flowers and finely-cut foliage. It prefers full sun and moderate water. Chamomile tea has been used since medieval times to cure headaches and relieve stress. More recently, Beatrix Potter had Peter Rabbit's mother give him chamomile tea after his stressful misadventures in Mr. McGregor's garden.

- French tarragon (*Artemesia dracunculus*) is a sprawling perennial with shiny, dark green, aromatic leaves. It prefers full sun and little water. Leaves are used in cooking meats and in sauces and sprigs may be added to white wine vinegar to create tarragon vinegar.

- Sorrel is a perennial with long arrow-shaped leaves. Common sorrel (*Rumex acetosa*) grows three feet tall whereas French sorrel (*Rumex scutatus*) grows to only eighteen inches. Both species taste like tangy spinach, though French sorrel is milder and with more lemon flavor. Sorrel leaves can be used to make soup, eaten in salads or as greens. Sorrel is more heat tolerant than spinach and produces throughout the growing season.

- Sage (*Salvia officinalis*) is the shrubby perennial sage used for culinary and medicinal purposes. Its aromatic wrinkled leaves are grayish-green on top and white and fuzzy underneath. Often used in dressings or in sauces, sage may also be added to salads. Sage tea was a traditional spring tonic—a mild laxative helping to clean the system of toxins built up in the body over the winter months. With its double meaning, sage is an emblem of age and wisdom. An adage says: "A man will live to aye (old age) / Who eats sage in May."

- Lovage (*Levisticum officinale*) is native to the eastern Mediterranean region. This perennial can be grown from seeds planted in the fall. Plants may reach three feet tall and wide. Its divided, glossy green leaves can be used in salads and added to soups and stews. Its greenish-yellow flowers will yield seeds in the fall that are valued for their celerylike flavor as an addition to homemade breads and cakes.

- Lemon balm (*Melissa officinalis*) is a perennial plant growing about two feet tall and eighteen inches wide. Its prolific seeds easily self-sow. The Greek word for bee is "Melissa," and bees certainly find it attractive. It is prized for its lemon-scented foliage, which may be added to cold drinks, fruit salads, and fish dishes.

Medicinally, it was used to make tea given to patients suffering from colds or fevers.

Plants I love in my garden today have a venerable history. They have been planted by gardeners for centuries and used for medicinal as well as culinary purposes. Their long and useful heritage adds an element of richness, and I see my garden with a new perspective.

~

CHAPTER THREE

~

*Flowering Plants*

# Ivy Geraniums
## (Pelargonium peltatum)

~

When my husband, two daughters and I moved to Marin County, my father sent us a housewarming present—a half-dozen ivy geranium plants, wrapped in plastic and mailed from Denver, Colorado.

At that time, my parents' home was festooned in ivy geraniums throughout the summer months. Each spring, my dad planted hundreds of them in window boxes not only under each window, but over the garage doors and in hanging baskets leading to the front door. The spectacular floral show received home beautification awards and was featured in local newspapers.

My father was inspired by the window boxes he knew growing up in the Netherlands. Ivy, balcony, or trailing geraniums are used in window boxes throughout Europe. In the years just following the war in Bosnia, I saw them in window boxes outside Sarajevo—the first signs of color heralding a return to normalcy.

In the San Francisco Bay area, with its moderate, Mediterranean climate, ivy geraniums (*Pelargonium peltatum*) grow year-round. I planted our housewarming presents in one container for our kitchen deck and three more containers for the lower deck in our backyard. I used commercial potting soil. It is fast-draining, for ivy geraniums do not like wet roots. However, as the water drains through the soil, it removes nutrients. My ivy geraniums do best when I add a

*~ Flowering Plants ~*

splash of liquid fertilizer to the watering can when I water them every week or so.

The container on our kitchen deck was only eighteen inches high. The ivy geranium was soon trailing on the deck. I found a metal stand for the container and now the plant happily grows three feet long before I trim it back. Over the years, the ivy geraniums became root-bound in their pots and, as a result, flowered even more profusely. Then disaster struck. The gate to our backyard was left open and neighborhood deer enjoyed a nocturnal feast. By morning, the geraniums on our lower deck had been decimated.

The good news is that ivy geraniums can be divided. I spread newspapers on the kitchen deck and removed the large surviving geranium from its pot. Delicately, I tried to pry it into sections. When that failed, I used a knife. I replanted one section in its pot and planted the others in the emptied containers on the lower deck.

Of those, two of the three newly-potted plants survived and are flourishing. They are in large containers and it will take a while for the plants to grow large enough to flower as lavishly as their predecessors. The third plant is entertaining some unexpected competition: lobelia have volunteered in the container and the geranium plant is buried in electric purple blooms. A single lobelia has sprouted in one of the other containers and the combination of pink geraniums and purple lobelia is so attractive I may move a few lobelia into the other containers and make it intentional.

To promote continuous bloom, ivy geraniums should be deadheaded. The blossoms' stems stretch out as long as six inches and should be broken off at the base. (The seed pod looks something like the bill of a stork—*pelargos* in Greek—after which the genus, *Pelargonium*, is named.) After a few weeks of inattention and neglect, in an exercise so repetitive it became a meditation, I broke off over two hundred spent blooms from the plant on our kitchen deck.

Microclimates exist even in the limited spaces of our decks. I have found that the ivy geraniums prefer to have some shade during the day. That is to say, the ivy geranium in full sun down below is not faring as well as the others. The ideal seems to be morning sun, afternoon shade, in a spot protected from the wind.

Ivy geraniums are tough and forgiving. Over the years, mine have tolerated neglect and drought. The drought, of course, was my failure to water them for weeks on end during summer. Their leaves turned brown and shriveled. However, once I resumed caring for them, added water and picked off their crispy leaves, they grew vigorously once again. During winter I ignore them; the rain takes over watering and flowers resume in the spring.

My father has passed away. One of his gifts to me was a love for gardening: the work of planting and caring for plants. He also bequeathed me a fascination about the plants themselves, their history and uses, above and beyond their natural beauty. Every time I see ivy geraniums—wherever they are—they remind me of my father's flowering housewarming gift.

# Shy Cyclamen

~

The pink and white flowers bend forward shyly on their slender stems. The stems rise naked from stone outcrops, a niche in the root of an ancient olive tree, or in happy profusion in the rich soil under a carob tree. Their dark green leaves will unfold later. These are wild cyclamen, growing in my Mediterranean garden in Greece.

In my Mediterranean garden in Marin County, I also have cyclamen, growing under the fragrant leaves of *Salvia clevelandii*. They are not a wild species. I planted a pot of cyclamen originally given to me in the early fall by my mother-in-law. When the blooms faded, the foliage was still flourishing, so I planted it outside. Over several years, it has spread by self-sowing seeds until it occupies an area adjacent to a garden bench.

According to the Cyclamen Society, an international society of cyclamen enthusiasts and scientists based in England, there are twenty species of cyclamen. Native to Europe and Mediterranean climates, their range extends from North Africa through Turkey, Greece, France and Switzerland to Slovakia.

Belonging to the primrose family, the relatively small genus of *Cyclamen* includes species that bloom every month of the year. The species growing in my garden in the southern Peloponnese is *Cyclamen graecum*. It is one of the fall-flowering species. The cyclamen in my Marin garden is a cultivar of *Cyclamen persicum*, the species of cyclamen that is most often grown commercially. A popular house plant, available from florists and even grocery stores, *C. persicum* normally flowers in the spring, but can be forced to flower for the winter holidays using artificial light in greenhouses. Blossoms range from white to pink, rose, red and magenta. Although *C. persicum* will not tolerate frost, it has survived enthusiastically, sheltered under shrubs in my garden in San Rafael.

The foliage of cyclamen is interesting in itself. Leaves vary from arrow-shaped to heart-shaped to kidney-shaped to round, depending on the species. The dark green leaves often have intricate patterns, traced in light green, cream or silver. At least two commercially available cultivars, *C. hederifolium* 'Silver Cloud' and *C. graecum* 'Glyfada' have pure silver foliage.

Fall-blooming species brighten the garden when summer flowers have faded. Early spring-blooming species are among the first flowers to appear, accompanying crocus and hellebores. For summer-blooming cyclamen, *Cyclamen purpurascens* flowers between June and September. This hardy species originates in Switzerland and Austria and grows in deciduous or partly evergreen woods up to 4,260 feet (1,300 meters). Its range extends the furthest north of any cyclamen species and it can tolerate temperatures as low as -19 degrees F. (-28 degrees C.), if blanketed by snow.

All parts of cyclamen are inedible by humans. However, pigs enjoy them, giving rise to their common name sowbread. Other, more attractive, common names include Persian Violet and Poor Man's Orchid.

Medicinal uses for cyclamen were first recorded by Dioscorides, a Greek surgeon in the first century C.E. According to his manuscripts, the root purges and cleanses the skin; it cures blemishes and boils; used alone or with honey,

*~ Flowering Plants ~*

it heals wounds; as a plaster it does good to a sunburned face; and it makes hair grow again.

Caring for cyclamen is easy. Indoors, cyclamen prefer temperatures around 55 degrees F. (12 degrees C.) and indirect sun. Pots should be allowed to dry between watering and saucers should be emptied after watering. Excess heat and overwatering are the most common ways to kill cyclamen. Like many Mediterranean natives, fall- and spring-flowering cyclamen have a dormant period during the summer months. *C. purpurascens* flowers in the summer, going dormant in winter. During dormancy, plants lose their leaves and stop growing. Houseplants should be put in a dry spot until fall. Outside plants do not require summer water; they prefer filtered sun and good drainage.

Cyclamen produce seed and will spread by self-sowing. They grow from tubers, which like potatoes, may be divided and propagated, providing each piece has a growth eye and a root region.

In my Marin garden, having moved successfully from indoors to outside, the cyclamen on their slender stems— shy no more— continued to delight me year after year.

# Low-water Succulents

~

Next to the front door of my house in Marin, a jade plant flourishes in a large pot. Jade plants are also known as money plants because their thick round leaves resemble coins. According to practitioners of feng-shui, this welcoming plant in the entryway will bring prosperity to the home owner.

Jade plants are just one type of succulent. More than sixty plant families include plants with succulent characteristics, distributed among three hundred genera and thousands of species.

For the water-conscious gardener, succulents may make an ideal contribution to the garden. Their varied textures, shapes and sizes will enhance the garden's design. Some succulents can contribute colorful flowers, others add striking foliage or sculptural forms. They may be planted in decorative pots, borders, or in the hard-to-water corners of the garden.

A succulent requires little or infrequent water because it is able to store water. Succulents are divided into those that store water in their leaves, stems or roots. Succulents that store water in their leaves often have thick, fleshy leaves covered with a tough skin, such as aloe vera. Plants that store water in their trunk often have small branches and leaves. Cacti are examples of stem succulents: their leaves have been reduced to spines. Other plants store water in their leaves and stems, for example jade plants. Geophytes, plants that die back during part of the year to their bulbs, tuberous roots, corms or rhizomes, are also considered succulents. Amaryllis, bromeliads and hyacinths are example of this type of succulent. Epiphytes, plants that live in the air, unattached to the ground, are succulents that depend on their ability to store water obtained from rain and fog. Some succulents are highly tolerant of salt and other chemicals and can live along the sea coast, in dry lakes or in highly polluted soil.

Other attributes that help succulents conserve water include:

- leaves that are cylindrical or spherical in shape, reduced in size, or absent
- fewer stomata (the openings in the leaves that allow transpiration)
- form of growth that is compact, columnar or spherical
- shallow roots to absorb moisture from light rain or heavy dew
- waxy, hairy or spiny outer surfaces that create humid micro-habitats, reducing air movement and water loss.

Small succulents may be used effectively as accents in the garden. For example, sedum or stone crop may be used as edging or even planted between paving stones or along foot paths.

Sansevieria—otherwise known as snake plant or mother-in-law's tongue—is a plant I remember from my childhood. Now I understand that this undemanding plant can tolerate low light, high or low heat, and erratic watering. Although I never really liked its long, knife-like leaves, it easily provided some green and life to otherwise sterile apartments. Sansevieria will thrive outdoors in a Mediterranean climate and its stiff straight leaves can add welcome contrast to soft, flowering borders.

Echeveria is a large genus of succulents characterized by lovely rosettes of fleshy leaves. They reproduce freely by offsets, tiny plants that grow around the edge of the mother plant. One of the most popular is *Echeveria secunda*, also known as Hen and Chicks. Depending on the species, Echeverias may be green, gray, silver, violet or even rose-hued. They are grown mostly for their foliage, although some species and cultivars develop stalks with flowers that are also quite attractive, for example *Echeveria* 'Blue Curl.'

Kalanchoes are succulents with showy flowers that can add a bright splash to the drought-tolerant garden.

Yucca trees store water in their trunks. With their interesting forms, they may serve as point-of-interest specimen plants.

Another very effective specimen plant is agave, which can grow to immense size in Mediterranean climates, ten feet across or more. Also called century plants, they look like enormous pieces of living sculpture and may thrive for many years. Eventually, the agave will produce a tall stalk with flowers. After the plant flowers once, it will die.

Succulents tend to reproduce very easily: a stalk, or even a leaf of a plant, may root itself and grow into a new plant. Some succulents, such as ice plant, have become invasive species in California.

In my garden in Greece, I have fallen in love with a low-growing succulent with pink, aster-like flowers: *Aptenia cordifolia*. This South African native is a relative of the ice plant, though not invasive. In the Byzantine fortress town of Monemvasia, residents grow *Aptenia cordifolia* on ledges and it trails down walls, bright pink blossoms splashing color against beige stone. I grow it in raised beds where it is just beginning to work its way over the edges. Under some of my olive trees, its light green leaves form a dense mat.

One of my favorite succulents is an *Aeonium*. This Mediterranean native grows about two feet tall, with rosettes of fleshy leaves. The rosettes of *Aeonium* 'Zwartkop' are very dark—almost black—as its name suggests. I first saw it in the garden of a large estate. As I exclaimed over it, an irreverent friend broke off a branch and handed it to me. I took it home and planted it. Over the years, it has demonstrated ability to survive despite near total neglect. Too much water is its main enemy. The more I ignore it, the more it thrives. Its dark foliage creates a wonderful contrast to the green and gray leaves of other plants in my garden. I have shared pieces of it with several friends, who have all grown it successfully.

Succulents themselves are the friends of low-water gardens—especially mine.

# *Experiencing Euphorbia*

~

In my friend's Tiburon garden, Mediterranean spurge spreads across a shaded hillside. When I admired their chartreuse flower bracts, my friend suggested I dig up a few young plants and take them home. "I put in two small plants a few years ago, and now look at this," she gestured widely with her arms.

Also known as *Euphorbia characias*, with subspecies *wulfenii* (from Turkey and the Balkans) and *characias* (from Portugal and Spain), Mediterranean spurge is native to the Mediterranean region and thrives in the San Francisco Bay area's Mediterranean climate.

The genus *Euphorbia* comprises over 2,100 species: just over half are succulents, some resembling cacti with tall branches covered with spines. Succulent euphorbias are native to north and south Africa and the Middle East. The remaining 45 percent are not true succulents and include such plants as popular Christmas poinsettias. All euphorbias are characterized by their white, milky sap. The sap contains toxic terpene esters, which can irritate the skin and damage eyes, so take care when cutting or handling them. However, the plants also have medicinal properties: *Euphorbia pekinensis* is one of the fifty fundamental herbs in Chinese medicine. Carolus Linnaeus assigned the name *Euphorbia* to the genus in honor of the Greek physician Euphorbus. Over two thousand years ago, Euphorbus reportedly used one of the species, possibly Russian spurge, as an herbal remedy to cure King Juba II of Numidia of a swollen belly.

With its slender, fleshy, blue-green leaves and chartreuse, cushion-shaped bracts, Mediterranean spurge grows from two to five feet tall, two to three feet wide, and makes an attractive addition to a garden border. A plentiful self-seeder, it can also be used as a groundcover. It blooms in spring and early summer, then tends to fade into the background by mid-summer. Its evergreen foliage remains attractive year-round. The flowers are insignificant and have no petals. It is bracts, that is modified leaves, that add dimension and color to the flowers. The bracts contain nectar glands that attract pollinators.

While driving along a country road in Greece, I was struck by the number of Mediterranean spurge I saw. They grow wild on the rocky hillsides here. Only drought resistant plants survive in the hot, harsh environment. The main requirement of this hardy plant is well-drained soil. Heavy soil may cause its roots to rot. Popular among gardeners in the southern Mediterranean for generations, *Euphorbia charcarias* is adapted to a variety of conditions and can tolerate temperatures below 0 degrees F. (-17.7 degrees C.), as long as the soil remains dry. Although it has adapted to difficult conditions, in the friendlier conditions of a garden, it will thrive.

The influential garden designer Gertrude Jekyll (1843-1932) referred to Mediterranean spurge as "one of the grandest and most pictorial of plants." To fill different niches in the garden, a number of cultivars have been developed, including 'Ember Queen' with variegated foliage, the compact 'Humpty Dumpty,' the strikingly blue 'Jade Dragon,' and the robust 'John Tomlinson' with spherical bracts sixteen inches in diameter. The related species *Euphorbia amygdaloides* var. *robbiae* is well adapted to dry shade. Especially useful as a ground cover, its glossy dark green leaves form a spreading mound. In the spring, panicles of yellow flowers seem to float above the leaves. Topping the list of purple-leaved perennials is *Euphorbia amygdaloides purpurea*, a sun-loving plant that contrasts spectacularly with spring's bright greens. (Not all *Euphorbias* are benign: *Euphorbia esula*, *Euphorbia oblongata*, and *Euphorbia terracina* are on the California Invasive Plant Inventory and should be avoided.)

Having gratefully accepted my friend's garden gift, I have planted the shoots of Mediterranean spurge in my own garden in Marin. As they grow, I will think of my friend—and the special bond gardens foster.

# Tending Roses in January

~

What is it about roses that is so endlessly fascinating? Perhaps it is their myriad petals—or perhaps their myriad forms: hybrid teas, floribunda, miniature, bush, old, wild, rambling, climbing. Or perhaps it is their unparalleled fragrance.

Our Mediterranean climate is well-suited to growing roses, assuming one's garden has a protected space with five or six hours of sun a day. Roses require sufficient sun to thrive.

January is the time of year when bare root roses are available at local nurseries. I am thinking of planting a new rosebush in a sunny spot as a specimen plant: I can see a large bush of yellow roses there. But before I plant another one, I will tend to my existing roses.

First, I will go through my rose bed and pick all the old leaves off the plants. The next few months, rose plants should go dormant, resting and getting ready to grow again in spring. If the rose plant is not supporting those last, clinging leaves, it will become dormant more quickly. Similarly, I will pull the petals from the faded flowers, but I will not cut them off. By leaving them on the plant, I encourage it to form rose hips—and then go dormant. Later on, I can gather the rose hips and use them to make tea.

I have several roses that are budded roses, that is, flowering canes grafted onto root stock. January is a good time to prune them. I will not prune my miniature rose bush, or the ramblers down in the corner of the garden (those not grafted onto root stock) because they bloom on current growth. If I prune them now, I will be cutting off this season's potential blooms.

For the others, I will prune off the dead branches, twiggy growth and crossing branches. Since I have removed the leaves, I can more easily see the skeleton of the plant and decide how I want to encourage it to grow. I cut one-quarter inch above a bud and slant the cut downwards away from the bud, so rainwater will drain off. I look carefully at the bud and consider the future shape of the bush: buds facing outward away from the center of the plant will increase the width of the plant as they grow. Buds facing inward toward the center of the plant will create a more compact shape. I remove one-third to one-half of the plant. Then I spray each rose with dormant oil to eliminate pests.

When I have finished pruning, I pick up all the leaves and petals and dispose of them. This act of good garden hygiene prevents pests developing in the discarded foliage, pests that would be well-positioned to attack my plants in spring.

Now for my new rose bush. At the nursery, I will examine the bare root roses—looking a lot like brown sticks—and choose one with several healthy canes growing above the bud union, the location at the base of the plant where a bud producing blooming canes was grafted onto the rootstock. I will also look for a substantial bundle of roots to support my plant. Since the plants have no leaves or flowers, I have to rely on the little metal tag attached to one of the canes to tell me which rose I am buying. Although the nursery may be selling plants dipped in wax, I will not consider buying any of them. The wax keeps the plants from drying out during shipment, but it also prevents the plants from breathing properly once they are planted.

~ *Flowering Plants* ~

Before I plant my new rose, I will trim off any broken roots and dead twigs and soak the entire plant for twenty-four hours in a bucket of water to rehydrate it. By adding one cup of household bleach to five gallons of water, I can kill any microbes the plant is carrying. I will be particularly industrious in digging a hole large enough to spread the roots out nicely. I like the old saw "put a fifty-cent plant in a five-dollar hole" to describe relative dimensions. Before I put any dirt back in the hole, I will mix it with compost from my compost pile. Since the soil in my garden is clay—that is, composed of a lot of small particles that clump together—mixing in compost lightens it and allows it to drain better.

In the bottom of the hole, I will build a cone of my newly mixed soil, high enough so that when I put the plant on it, the bud union will be about three inches above ground. I will spread its bare roots over the mound so they will support the plant from all directions. Then I will fill in the rest of the soil mixture, carefully tamping it down. I will add mulch around the stem of the plant, covering the bud union to keep it from drying out. The mulch should be removed after six weeks. In the next few months, the mound of soil under the rose will compact and the plant will sink, so the bud union will be just above the ground. I will build a small dike around the plant and I will water it well—my father used to call it "puddling in."

Our winter rains will probably keep my new rose plant watered, but if we have a dry spell, I will make sure to keep the plant moist. By spring, it will be ready to grow, and if I have purchased a budded rose, it should bloom the first year. If I have bought a rose growing on its own roots, I will not expect any blossoms: its job this first year is to develop healthy roots and become established. In either case, I anticipate many beautiful blooms in years to come.

# Plant California Native Bulbs in Autumn

~

Fragile fairy lanterns, pale purple *brodiaea*, creamy mariposa lilies—all are California natives which grow from bulbs or corms.

Flowers synonymous with spring—iris, tulips, trillium—propagate by division of underground structures. Bulbs are modified leaf bases enclosing buds. Corms and rhizomes are thickened stems.

Earliest in the spring, trillium bloom. As their name suggests, their leaves grow in a three-leafed whorl, topped by a maroon or white flower with three petals. They prefer a shady part of the garden and are comfortable among ferns and azaleas. Growing from a single rhizome, trillium will slowly increase into a clump.

Mid-spring, iris show their colors. Eleven species of Pacific Coast iris form their own group within the iris genus. California native iris reputedly spread through creeping rhizomes to form clumps that can be divided during wet winter months. Although the Douglas iris, *Iris douglasiana*, I planted in my garden have not spread much, I trust they will live up to their reputation. Douglas iris range from pale to dark purple in color. Other forms of iris have been crossed with this species to produce Pacific Coast Hybrids, or PCH. They cover a broad palette of colors, from copper to pink, bright yellow to maroon.

Fairy lanterns bloom beginning in March. The white fairy lantern or globe tulip, *Calochortus albus*, is widespread

~ *Flowering Plants* ~

in woodlands from San Francisco Bay south through the Sierra foothills. The golden globe tulip, *C. amabilis*, is more compact and has rich yellow blooms. The *Calochortus* genus also includes the mariposa lily, of which there are at least a dozen species of California natives. They range in habitat from grasslands to chaparral, from coastal foothills to low deserts.

Another genus with a number of native California species is *Brodiaea*, or harvest lily. These grow from corms in a variety of soils, from heavy adobe to mountain meadows. During the summer, they need to rest and therefore require no water. *Brodiaea* flowers are a cluster of glossy blue or purple funnels at the top of a stem. There are low-growing *Brodiaea* such as *B. nana* with pale blue flowers that tolerate adobe soil. Other *Brodiaea* grow tall: stately *B. californica* shows purple blooms from May to July.

Plants which used to be considered *Brodiaea* have now been separated into their own genus. These close relatives include the wild hyacinth and blue dicks, now called *Dichelostemmas*, and Ithuriel's Spear and Milk Lily, now called *Triteleias*. *Dichelostemmas* include the firecracker flower, *D. ida-maia*, an eye-catching cluster of red and green flowers which may grow up to three feet high. Others are blue dicks, *D. capitatum* and the wild hyacinth. *D. multiflorum*. All grow well in mixed bulb borders. Ithuriel's Spear, *Triteleia laxa*, is the most common and easiest to grow. Its purple flowers burst from stiff, leafless two-foot stalks.

California has many native lilies. They fall into two groups: those with creeping rhizomatous bulbs that require moisture year-round and those with large single bulbs that need a dry summer to rest. The leopard lily, *Lilium pardalinum*, has orange or red-orange flowers with brown spots in a graceful, recurved form. It requires sufficient water year-round. In its native habitat, it is widespread along streams and in wet meadows. One of the easiest native lilies to grow in the garden, over time leopard lilies will naturalize and form colonies. By contrast, the Humboldt lily, *L. humboldtii*, requires only occasional summer water. It has a similar spotted pattern on yellow-orange petals and blooms midsummer.

These are just some of the native California plants that grow from bulbs, corms and rhizomes. Fall is the best season to plant them, although as plants from nurseries, they may be planted at other times of year. The reward will be splashes of garden color from native Californians from early spring through summer.

CHAPTER FOUR

*Shrubs and Trees*

# *Ceanothus Blue*

~

Driving through Tiburon, I passed a small tree covered in purple blossoms. It was a ceanothus, possibly *Ceanothus arboreus*, that is tree ceanothus, which grows either as a dense shrub or can be pruned to develop one main trunk. Ceanothus is native to the western United States and, besides being beautiful in spring covered with purple or white blossoms, has adapted to tolerate a wide variety of climates. It is also known as wild lilac, with blossoms in a similar, miniature form.

    Over thirty species of *Ceanothus* grow in many shapes and sizes, though all can be classified as perennial shrubs. With their showy flowers, ceanothus attract hummingbirds and butterflies. They are a fine addition to a habitat garden. In my garden, consciously emphasizing natives and habitat-creating plants, I have planted four different species, for different purposes.

    Ceanothus do not require summer water, which make them appealing for that reason alone. In fact, their greatest enemy is over-watering and they may succumb to the water mold Phytophthora. They are therefore suitable for planting under oaks, a major consideration in my garden. Under a venerable old oak in our lower garden, I have planted *C. griseus horizontalis* 'Carmel Creeper.' Its shiny dark-green round leaves are what first attracted me. The fact that it is blooming with tiny purple panicles at the end of February adds to its charm. My garden is separated into an upper and lower section by a tall fence. The upper garden is open

~ *Shrubs and Trees* ~

to the deer that are frequent visitors. The lower garden is protected from their grazing. Deer like to eat various varieties of *C. griseus,* including Carmel Creeper, so I planted it inside the fence.

Under another oak in the lower garden, I planted *C. hearstiorum.* This flat-growing species was discovered on the grounds of Hearst Castle and is reputed to be an endangered species. I could not resist the opportunity to plant some in my garden, although it is considered an undependable performer. But so far, so good. It grows in a star shape and has spread quickly across the slope under the oak. It is not a thick ground cover and some weeds do appear between its branches, but I am very happy with it. It will be blooming soon.

In the upper garden, I recently planted a strip of garden beside steps that lead up to an oak tree growing next to our street. Here, I had to consider plants that do not appeal to deer. Already in place were fortnight lilies, *Dietes,* with their stiff, swordlike leaves, divisions of lilies from elsewhere in the garden. Likewise, I had planted clumps of sword ferns, also taken from a mother plant along this side of the house. I lined the steps with variegated-leafed allium. Against the fence, I planted two different varieties of ceanothus that have prickly holly-type leaves and so do not appeal to deer. As a background shrub, I chose *C. thyrsiflorus* 'Skylark.' The deer have avoided it to date. It may grow up to six feet tall and five feet wide.

Several varieties of ceanothus are also effectively used on slopes for erosion control. On my slope, I planted a prostrate ceanothus with small, leathery leaves. It is a perfect candidate for covering a steep, dry open bank. Although its leaves are not prickly, they are not very succulent, so I am hoping the deer will choose something else for snacks.

Ceanothus are susceptible to several pests. One of the most common—and quite serious—can be the ceanothus stem gall moth that causes spindle-shaped swellings (galls). Infestation may cause serious dieback. Spring is the time of year to look for these swellings. Clip them off and dispose of them. It is very important not to drop them on the ground—moths will emerge. Another pest is the lace bug (*Ceanothus tingids*). Ceanothus may also be attacked by oyster shell scale, which unfortunately is not easy to control.

Ceanothus are relatively short-lived shrubs—between four and ten years. They cannot compete against some invasive species. In a passage in her book *Gardening with a Wild Heart*, Judith Lowry imagines a day when our native ceanothus have been replaced by aggressive, invasive broom: "There will be no honey-sweet fragrance emanating from fragile ceanothus blossoms, no strange dry black seeds dropping in midsummer. Tortoiseshell butterflies will not be laying eggs on shiny ceanothus leaves, nor will the ceanothus moth make its cocoons, prized rattles for traditional dances. There will be no swishing the blossoms in a bucket of water to make suds to wash with, as the Pomo did, and wreaths made for the Strawberry Festival will no longer include ceanothus. There will just be yellow." That would be a sad day indeed.

Ceanothus are worthy additions to our gardens as native, drought-tolerant, deer-resistant (some species) shrubs, with flowers attractive to insects and birds as well as to us. At least in my garden, ceanothus will not disappear.

# *Zauschneria aka Epilobium*

~

A few years ago, while at the annual native plant sale sponsored by the California Native Plant Society at Merritt College in the East Bay, I purchased two *Zauschneria* plants, also known as California Fuchsia. One was the common *Zauschneria californica* with threadlike gray leaves and narrow red trumpet-like flowers, the other was *Zauschneria latifolium*, with broader, ovate gray-green leaves and somewhat larger, showier red blooms.

I chose them for several reasons. As I continue working to develop my garden as a habitat attractive to birds, I seek plants for the sustenance they offer different species. *Zauschnerias'* bright red flowers are exceptionally attractive to hummingbirds and, in fact, one of the common names of this perennial is Hummingbird Trumpet. If I allow it to go to seed—as I always do because it would be too much trouble to deadhead the prolific blooms—the seeds, surrounded by white fluff, provide a feast for goldfinches and other songbirds.

Another reason I chose to plant *Zauschneria* is that it self-propagates. Some folks consider it rampant and invasive. But that is why I planted it. I am striving for a wild and natural effect in that section of my garden and I welcome the new shoots as they spread. Seeds that escape the birds' attention easily germinate. They also commonly spread by rhizomes along their roots, filling in gaps between other plants. It always pleases me to see the little gray threads of growth heralding a new arrival.

The wide-spreading roots that may grow into new plants are also very effective at seeking water. *Zauschnerias* are drought-tolerant. After the first summer needed to establish themselves, they need little additional water. There is some variation between species, however, *Z. latifolia* requiring more water than *Z. californica*.

In addition, the soil in my lower garden is very poor, but this has not seemed to discourage these hardy plants.

They are reputed to be deer resistant, but in *Gardening with a Wild Heart*, Judith Lowry notes that "California fuchsia, *Epilobium canum*, ranks high on several deer-resistant lists, yet on a recent job, it was munched almost to the point of no return as soon as we walked away." I cannot say. Mine are protected by a high fence. However, on the occasions when deer have entered that section of my garden, the *Zauschnerias* have not suffered, apparently ranking lower among deer's preferred foods than roses, lemons and geraniums.

Although *Zauschnerias* may grow to be over two feet tall, mine have stayed much shorter, not more than twelve inches high. They flower in the fall, adding an exuberant dash of color when not much else in my garden is in bloom. By Christmas, however, the flowers are gone. Now is the time to cut it back, or as some gardeners recommend, to "mow it down." By cutting back the woody growth, the plant will grow fuller in the spring. In his *Complete Garden Guide to the Perennials of California*, Glenn Keator suggests that "Since these are of only moderate height, they are best for the middle part of a mixed border, as a rank ground cover, in front of drought-tolerant chaparral shrubs, or in an expansive rock garden."

I have always loved the name *Zauschneria*. Once I finally sounded it out, it pleased me to say it out loud. Being the only plant besides zinnia that I knew starting with "z," it was easy to remember. It was named after Johann Baptista Josef Zauschner (1737–1799), a professor of medicine and botany in Prague. My attempts to learn more about how a plant native to California came to the attention of a professor in Prague proved fruitless. I wanted to know why one of my favorite garden plants carried his name. But it seems that the plant bearing his name may have been his greatest, if not only, legacy.

It saddened me to learn that botanical studies have eliminated *Zauschneria* as a distinctive genus. It is now placed within the genus *Epilobium*. For some reason, this new name is harder for me to remember. However, another of my favorite plants, one that I have never even considered growing in my garden, is a member of the genus *Epilobium*: fireweed. My low-growing gray plants do not bear the slightest resemblance to these proud, tall green spikes of electric red-purple flowers that are the first to germinate in a fire-ravaged forest. But if my plants' name *Zauschneria* had to be eliminated, I am pleased to learn they have such attractive relatives.

# Spiny Barberries

~

For years, I have noticed barberries in municipal plantings, and, perhaps for that reason alone, dismissed them from my garden. Or maybe barberry's spiny branches repelled me.

However, I am always looking for plants that may flourish in my deer-accessible garden. The spiny branches that repelled me also effectively repel deer. And recently I learned that barberry is used as a medicinal herb in both Chinese and Western traditions. This additional information tipped the balance, and I have begun researching which species of barberry would best fit my garden.

In many ways, barberry is an attractive plant. The various species of *Berberis* have yellow flowers in spring. By fall, they are covered with red or dark purple berries, very popular with birds; the species described below are especially prolific. Foliage ranges from various shades of green to red, magenta, and bronze. Some species are deciduous; others maintain their leaves year-round. They are exceptionally tough plants, surviving under harsh weather conditions and in poor soil. These versatile shrubs are hardy in all climate zones.

The genus *Berberis* is a member of the family Berberidaceae, which contains both shrubs and herbaceous perennials. *Nandina*, known as heavenly bamboo, is also a member of this family. *Vancouveria*, including the inside-out flower, and *Epimedium*, such as bishop's hat, are examples of the family's herbaceous perennials.

~ *Shrubs and Trees* ~

In terms of general garden design considerations—color, texture and form—barberries have much to offer. In my garden, I have many plants with gray-green leaves, lavender and rosemaries, Zauschnerias (*Epilobium*) and Santolinas. I am considering planting a Darwin barberry (*Berberis darwinii*) for its dark evergreen, holly-like leaves. Its orange-yellow flowers are reputed to be so thick along the branches that it will be difficult to see the foliage in spring. I imagine the contrast of the orange-yellow flower with my deep-purple Spanish lavender would be spectacular. In fall, the Darwin barberry's dark purple berries would add to the habitat I am establishing to attract birds to our garden. We have several oak trees in our garden, and Darwin's barberry is well-suited to planting under them. As this barberry spreads by underground runners, I will plan carefully before I plant.

For a barrier hedge, I am considering Wilson barberry (*B. wilsoniae*). It may grow to six feet high and equally wide, but may be trimmed shorter. Its fine leaves are light green, and its small yellow flowers grow in dense clusters. Berries are coral to salmon red. *B. wilsoniae* is also a medicinal herb. In traditional Chinese medicine, the root, bark, berries and leaves of *B. wilsoniae*, or *San ke zhen*, are used to stimulate digestion and reduce inflammation, among other things. For more about barberry's use as an herbal medicine in both Eastern and Western traditions, Peter Holmes' book *The Energetics of Western Herbs* is fascinating and informative.

For an additional color contrast, I am considering barberries with dark red leaves. Several varieties of Japanese barberry (*B. thunbergii* 'Atropurpurea') is bronze-red to purplish-red all summer. I would plant it in a sunny spot to make sure the leaves develop their full color. *B. thunbergii*

'Cherry Bomb' is another choice for a shrub with red leaves; it grows to about four feet in height. For a smaller splash of red, I could choose *B. thunbergii* 'Crimson Pygmy'; it generally grows only one and a half feet tall.

The foliage and berries of *Berberis* will add much to my garden. The spines on their branches, which will deter the deer, ensure they survive.

# *Coyote Bush*

~

At an author event at Habitat Books in Sausalito (sadly now closed), Judith Lowry of Larner Seeds once extolled the attributes of coyote bush. I had seen this California native, with its small green leaves and cottony seeds, along the trails of Mt. Tam and Point Reyes, but had never considered planting it in my garden. After listening to what Lowry had to say, I now intend to plant several.

In the wild, coyote bush (*Baccharis*) plays various roles. In an oak woodland community, coyote bush serves as a nurse plant, sheltering young oaks until they are strong enough to survive without its protection. The coastal scrub community of Marin County consists of an evergreen shrub layer of which coyote bush is a common element. This vegetation type occurs on the lower slopes of hills and bluffs along our foggy coast.

In the garden, coyote bush can also play a number of roles. As a woody, mature shrub, it creates a habitat for birds. In Lowry's book *Gardening with a Wild Heart*, she says, "Some birds, like wrentits and white-crowned sparrows, live their whole lives in coyote bush, finding there all they need for perching, nesting, breeding, eating, and resting." Alternatively, it can be cut to the ground when young to regrow into a shapely, herbaceous mound. Lowry uses coyote bush as keynote plant in her own garden, repeating it in several locations to develop continuity in design. For a number of years, Lowry say it did not reseed. However, her coyote bushes are now doing so. On a large tract of agricultural land, coyote bushes could become a pest for that reason. However, in a domestic garden, reseeding is not a serious problem.

In Marjorie Schmidt's classic book, *Growing Native California Plants*, she describes one species of coyote bush, *Baccharis pilularis*, also known as Dwarf Chaparral Broom or Dwarf/prostrate Coyote Bush, as "an important bank and slope cover, useful on road cuts as well as in home gardens." In her comments entitled Estimate of Garden Value, she says, "Because of the popularity of *B. pilularis*, new forms have been selected for rich green leaf color and good performance. Some have a honey-like fragrance which attracts many butterflies....Two selected forms include *B. pilularis* 'Twin Peaks,' an old standby, and the newer *B. pilularis* 'Pigeon Point,' noted for its dark green foliage. Both are considered fire retardant and are not eaten by deer."

"Not eaten by deer" is a particularly important quality of coyote bush as far as I am concerned. For years, deer have stayed outside the fence of my lower garden. A month or so ago, one squeezed through a hole caused by a rotten wooden post. I repaired the fence, but having discovered the delicious plants in my garden, deer learned they could jump over the fence that had so long deterred them. Faced with the prospect of building a new higher fence or replacing my devoured plants, I have decided to replant with species distinctly unappealing to my uninvited guests. Continuing my research, I consulted Glen Keator's *Complete Garden Guide to the Native Shrubs of California*. Regarding dwarf/prostrate coyote bush, Keator recommends "periodic mowing or shearing of top growth to maintain both vigor and low stature."

He also informs that "Dwarf coyote bush is propagated exclusively from cuttings of the male plant, since the female form, when it goes to seed, creates masses of wind-blown, white-tufted, messy fruits. The male plant bears inconspicuous, innocuous heads of creamy disc flowers. Since seed-grown plants are unpredictable as to gender, cuttings are the only way to go. The dense, shiny green, small rounded leaves remain attractive throughout the year, a real plus in summer drought or winter wet. On warm days, leaves may become resinous and aromatic with a pleasing and subtle fragrance."

My constant quest is to develop my garden as a habitat for insects, butterflies, and birds. Adding coyote bush will further that objective.

The fragrance of the coyote bush is a plus in that regard. Planting several bushes this fall, while the ground is still warm, will give them a chance to get established before next summer's drought. I already anticipate the sweet-smelling benefits coyote bush will bring to my garden.

# Oleander: Toxic and Tough

~

Oleander is highly poisonous. According to the *California Master Gardener Handbook*, children can be poisoned by sucking on the flowers, chewing the leaves, or grilling food on skewers made from its branches. Even the fumes from burning oleander are hazardous. Oleander can cause illness and even death.

Why, then, do we plant it? We plant it for its other qualities: dark green foliage, long blooming season, and abundant pink or white or red flowers. It is a thick shrub that can be pruned early to form attractive single- or multi-stemmed small trees.

In the Southwest, it can be a living fence. In California, it is a favorite municipal planting. Planted for miles along highways, it turns strips of asphalt into gardens. Once established, it requires little water. It thrives in poor soil. It tolerates dry, sandy soil, as well as moist, clay soil and soil with high salt content. It prefers sun, but can be grown in shade, although plants produce fewer flowers in the shade. My experience is that, in our Mediterranean climate, oleander is hard to kill.

Oleander grows best where it doesn't freeze; however, there are frost-tolerant hybrids. A native of the Mediterranean region, it was cultivated in the valley of the Nile in 2500 B.C.E., according to historical documents. Oleander grows from sea level along the coast to 8,200 feet (2,500 meters) above sea level.

~ *Shrubs and Trees* ~

From the Mediterranean, it was carried through the Red Sea and Indian Ocean to the South Pacific and eventually to the Caribbean islands. In 1841, Joseph Osterman, a merchant, brought oleanders to Galveston, Texas, from Jamaica. Galveston is now called the "Oleander City" and has perhaps the most extensive collection of oleanders in the world.

It is cultivated throughout East Africa. In India, Hindu mourners place oleander blooms about the bodies of dead relatives. In Germany, potted oleanders are placed outside the kitchen window for good luck.

Late September and early October is the time to prune, so as not to inhibit spring growth. Pruning oleander to just above the leaf nodes will produce a bushier plant. From each cut, three new shoots will appear. To encourage a globe shape, after the new shoots grow for a while, each can be pruned again, yielding three more shoots per cut. Flowers grow on new wood, so a flower should appear at the tip of each shoot. Removing the shoots at the base of the flower clusters also promotes blooming. After the flowers have dropped, trim the tips of the stems.

Oleander is easy to propagate from cuttings. Either hard wood or tip cuttings may be used. Make cuttings about six inches long and remove the lower leaves. Place the cuttings in water. Roots will start growing from the bottom three leaf nodes. After the roots grow one to two inches long, transplant to well-drained soil. They should be kept moist, not wet, and in a mostly sunny location. Alternatively, cuttings can be dipped in root hormone and planted in sand.

Oleanders are subject to some pests:

- For aphids, spray bushes with horticultural oil in late spring.

- Oleander gall caused by the bacterium *Pseudomonas syringae* pv. Savastanoi can cause galls on twigs, branches, leaves, flowers and seed pods. The bacterium enters through leaf and blossom scars, wounds produced by pruning, frost injury and natural openings. Rain, sprinkler water and pruning tools can spread the bacterium from diseased to healthy plants (it is better not to use overhead sprinklers). Always dip pruning tools in disinfectant between cuts, and prune during the dry season.

- Dwarf varieties (commonly used for low borders, hedges and background plantings) are very prone to the bacterium, especially in partial shade.

Oleander hybrids have been bred over the years, and they are available with single and double flowers and in shades of coral and yellow, as well as many reds, pinks and white. Small varieties may be used as hedges, large varieties as lush, flowering screens. In my garden in Greece, I planted an oleander bush on each side of one entryway to my garden. I am pruning them to grow into low, wide bushes: their prolific pink and white blossoms will welcome my garden guests.

# *Bamboo*

*~*

Tall stems sway in the wind; sun shines through the rustling leaves, dappling the ground below. "Bamboo is an image of resilience, as is easily understood because of its supple nature . . . [I]ts hollow trunk metaphorically depicted the Zen principle of an empty heart (*mushin*)," according to Marc P. Keane in *Japanese Garden Design*.

Bamboo can add a feeling of grace and serenity to the garden—and an oriental tone. It can be used as a decorative element, a windbreak, or a privacy screen. It will prevent soil erosion and provide food for the table as well as forage for animals. Depending on its intended use in the garden, there are dozens of species to choose from.

But one should not plant bamboo without giving the matter sufficient thought. If you are going to grow bamboo, plan for containment! There are two main types: running and clumping. Running bamboo spreads by rhizomes that may grow two to three feet underground. These bamboos are hard to confine, even to pots. Clumping bamboos are much less aggressive. Their rhizomes tend to grow straight up stead of out, and the plant stays confined to a slow-growing clump.

Certain species of running bamboo can be extremely invasive. In the genuses *Arundinaria*, *Chimonobambusa*, and *Phyllostachys*, the underground stems grow varying distances from the parent plant before sending up shoots. If they are not controlled, they may eventually produce large groves.

According to the American Bamboo Society: "If bamboo has been planted without root barrier and is now growing where you don't want it, you have several choices. The choices all start out with digging a trench about three feet deep around the area where you want the bamboo to grow. You can then install root barrier, pour concrete at least three inches thick or fill the trench with loose gravel. If you choose root barrier or concrete, you should leave an inch or two above ground level to make it easier to find the roots that try to escape over the top of the barrier. If you choose the loose rock fill, you will have to use a sharp spade at the beginning of every growing season to cut down into the trench and sever any new roots that try to cross the trench. Rhizomes that have already extended outside their area can be dug up. If that isn't practical, continue to knock over all new shoots you see for the next few seasons, once the rhizomes are severed from the main plant, and the rhizomes will eventually die."

If you have a large space to fill, running bamboo may be a solution. For most of us, the answer is to choose a different genus of bamboo.

Clump bamboo, including the genuses *Banbusa*, *Chusquea*, *Fargesia*, and *Otatea*, have underground stems that grow only a short distance before sending up new stems. They form manageable clumps that expand slowly around the edges. To contain them completely, these bamboo may be grown in large pots or redwood boxes. Clump bamboo come in various shapes and hues. *Bambusa oldhamii* is known as the clumping giant timber bamboo and grows between fifteen and fifty-five feet tall. *Bambusa multiplex* 'Alphonse Karr' grows between eight and thirty-five feet and has culms (stems) brightly green and yellow striped. Buddha's Belly Bamboo, *B. ventricosa*, stays small when grown in containers and produces swollen culms that give it its name. Chinese Goddess Bamboo, *B. m. riviereorum*, has tiny, lacy fern-like leaves that grow on gracefully arching culms.

To propagate bamboo, dig up a clump of it, making sure to keep it moist and plant it immediately before it dries out. The best time to divide clumps for propagation is just before the growing season begins in the spring.

According to Phillip Cave in *Creating Japanese Gardens*, "Bamboos generally like a moisture-retentive soil with a reasonable clay and organic matter content, although the black bamboo (*Phyllostachys nigra*) colors up best in sandy soil." Bamboo should be watered during its fast-growing season in the spring. It also needs water if its leaves curl during a dry summer spell. Depending on the species, it may prefer anything from full sun to full shade. Leaves that drop can be left around the base of the plant to serve as mulch and provide the silica it will need for future growth.

Pests that attack bamboo include the bamboo mite and aphids. Gophers like to eat the shoots.

Humans also find bamboo shoots good to eat. Bamboo growers reportedly snack on them while working during the "shooting" season. Although some bamboos contain cyanogens and must be cooked before eating, this is generally not a problem with bamboos grown in temperate climates. Most can be eaten without cooking if they are not too bitter.

I love the atmosphere bamboo creates. But it can too easily run rampant. In my garden, bamboo will be confined to a large pot on a balcony. It will add an oriental accent—and I will not worry about its escape.

# *Redwoods as Garden Plants*

~

When I visited a friend near Graton in Sonoma County, we gazed in awe at the height of a stand of redwoods outside her front door. "This grove isn't a natural one," she explained. "It was planted about fifty years ago."

I was amazed; the trees appeared mature. She went on to explain that redwoods are fast-growing—three to five feet a year. In twenty-five years, they may reach seventy to ninety feet tall.

I had always appreciated them as part of the natural landscape along the coast, but had never thought about planting them in the garden.

In fact, *Sequoia sempervirens*, or coast redwood, is not confined to the coast. Although coast redwoods thrive in heavy coastal fog and fifty- to sixty-degree temperatures, they will grow in widely varying environments, including Fresno, California, and states such as Georgia, Florida and Arizona.

The coast redwood is the tallest of the world's trees, with some centuries-old specimens more than three hundred fifty feet high. In gardens, the coast redwood may grow fifty to one hundred feet high, with a branch span of twenty to thirty feet in width, so it is important to choose an appropriate location for this specimen tree. For example, redwoods planted under power lines may be deformed by necessary trimming. Or, as they grow, redwoods may obscure a neighbor's view and require periodic "windowing."

~ *Shrubs and Trees* ~

We have a redwood in our garden that requires windowing. It fits perfectly into a corner between bedroom and bathroom windows and, from an inside view, this single tree creates the feel of a forest. I called the previous owners of our house to ask when they planted it. "A few years after we built the house. Must have been in the early 1970s," came the reply. When we bought the house in the 1990s, the tree already towered above the two-story roof.

Ivy had overgrown the area under our redwood and was climbing up the trunk. With some difficulty, I pulled it all out. But I was unsure what to plant there instead.

In her essay, "Native Plants Under Redwoods," published in *Bay Area Gardening*, Virginia Havel points out that the needles and cones that naturally drop from redwoods contain resins called allelopaths that inhibit seed generation of other plants. To thrive under redwoods, plants must like shade and moisture and be resistant to allelopaths.

Havel suggests planting California natives such as redwood sorrel (*Oxalis oregana*), wild ginger (*Asarum caudatum*), redwood violet (*Viola sempervirens*) and false lily-of-the-valley (*Maianthemum dilatatum*). She suggests planting such bushes as coffeeberry (*Rhamnus californica*), huckleberry (*Vaccinium ovatum*) and wild azalea (*Rhododendron occidentale*).

I planted several clumps of sword ferns and redwood sorrel under our redwood. That was several years ago, and the redwood sorrel has spread by creeping rootstock all around the base of the tree. In the spring, the redwood sorrel sports pink and white flowers. Its leaves resemble shamrocks.

Traditionally, redwoods sold at nurseries were grown from seed. The species is tall, columnar or conical in form, with horizontal branches and drooping new growth.

Several cultivated varieties (cultivars) with specific color and growth characteristics are now available. 'Aptos Blue' maintains the typical form, with dense blue-green foliage. 'Adpressa' is smaller, slower-growing and hardier: twenty to thirty feet tall and ten to twenty feet across. 'Santa Cruz' has light green foliage, a soft texture and branches pointing slightly down. 'Prostrata' is a dwarf, spreading cultivar that may revert to upright form unless attentively pruned. 'Soquel' has bluish-green foliage that turns up at the tips. 'Filoli' and 'Woodside' are possibly identical varieties with intense blue foliage.

Redwoods have developed numerous survival techniques. When a fire burns through a forest, although the interior of the redwoods may be burned out, the trees will survive because of their extraordinarily thick and fibrous bark. In flooded areas where several feet of silt have been deposited, redwood trees have set out new root systems.

Redwood is remarkably unsusceptible to rot and decay, including root rot. Termites and ants find redwoods distasteful or possibly poisonous. If a redwood tree is knocked over, the limbs pointing up will grow into a line of trees. When a redwood has been cut down, a circle of trees will grow in a radius around the stump.

Redwood burls remain dormant as long as the tree is healthy. However, if the tree weakens or dies, shoots will soon appear from the burl. Burls are sold as houseplants for this reason. Keep a redwood burl in a shallow pan of water, and it will develop a fringe of feathery greens.

As a single specimen tree in our garden, the redwood tree grows perfectly in its unique space. It brings the coastal forest into our home.

## *Specimen Trees*

~

Specimen trees are incorporated in a garden because of their beautiful flowers, architectural shapes, ornamental bark, prolific perfume or outstanding foliage. Specimen trees also may be planted to commemorate important occasions—the birth of a child, a marriage, even a death. They are given pride of place, a special spot where the tree's attributes will be fully appreciated. The specimen tree should grab one's attention.

At the entrance to my property in Greece, I planted a species of Cassia tree that had been given to me by a friend. It was a living house-warming gift. My friend had dug out a shoot from her own tree, potted it and cared for it for several years, until it became a viable young tree.

It is well-suited to the Mediterranean climate, although it does appreciate additional water during the summer, even after it is established. Its spectacular yellow blossoms and medium size make it an excellent specimen tree. Because I was able to plant it in an open space along the footpath leading to my house, it enjoys full sun and can be easily seen and appreciated. When I planted it, I enriched the soil with some humus I had taken from the base of my carob tree.

In Greece, the rich humus that develops at the base of carob trees is commonly used to amend garden soil. Carob trees grow well in Mediterranean climates, without requiring any additional water. They also can be considered specimen trees, with their interesting carob pods. If properly pruned, they will provide comfortable year-round shade.

On my property, the single carob tree provides a screen between my property and my neighbor's. Carob trees grow large and require a large garden space. Carob pods are edible—they taste similar to chocolate—and can be ground up and used as a chocolate substitute.

In my garden in Marin, we had a small, flowering cherry tree that provided a focal point in spring with its delicate blossoms. Sadly, after a hard winter, it died. Thinking about replacing it, I have considered planting a persimmon tree. As specimen trees, persimmons can be considered purely ornamental: in the fall they lose their leaves and the fruit remains hanging on the bare branches, looking like orange Christmas-tree ornaments.

However, if one consumes those orange globes, persimmons could accurately be considered fruit trees. I wait until persimmons are fully ripe, then scoop out the sweet pudding-like pulp and add it to my morning fruit juice drink. Alternatively, the pulp can be added to steamed puddings or breads.

In spring, the tree's foliage emerges pale green. In summer, the leaves become thick and leathery, providing excellent shade. Depending on where you plant a persimmon tree in the garden, it could be used to provide architectural interest, fruit, shade or all three.

It may also provide a symbolic connection. While young, persimmons are bitter and inedible, but as they age, they become sweet and beneficial to mankind. In the famous painting by the 13th-century Chinese painter Mu Qi, "Six Persimmons," persimmons exemplify the progression from youth to age, as a symbol of the progression from bitterness to sweetness. As we age, we overcome rigidity and prejudice and attain compassion and sweetness.

My older daughter recently celebrated, somewhat reluctantly, her thirtieth birthday. She is in shock at being no longer in her twenties. My husband and I are in shock at having a thirty-year-old daughter. How old does that make us?

The persimmon tree has a message for us all. It may be the perfect reason to choose it as a replacement specimen tree, a birthday tree honoring my daughter that has a message for her parents, too.

~
CHAPTER FIVE
~

*Fruits of the Garden*

# *Pomegranates*

~

Every culture has its New Year's tradition: in Greece pomegranates are given to symbolize abundance and good luck. The proffered fruit may be fresh or in the form of silver, copper, or ceramic decorations.

Although pomegranate trees are native to the area stretching from Iran to the Himalayas in northern India, they have been cultivated throughout the Mediterranean region since ancient times. They figure in the Greek myth of Demeter and Persephone, and in the Egyptian myth of Isis and Osiris. In the Bible, Solomon sang of an "orchard of pomegranates" and the Koran refers to pomegranates as examples of God's good creations and as a fruit found in the Garden of Paradise.

The name pomegranate derives from the Latin *pomum*, meaning apple, and *granatus*, meaning seeded. Common names include "Chinese apples" and "wine apples" in Ireland. In Spanish, they are called *grenada*, the same word used for similarly-shaped hand grenades.

The pomegranate was brought to England as an exotic plant in the 1600s, but it was too cold there for the plant to set fruit. Undeterred, the English sent pomegranate stock to the American colonies, where it was cultivated successfully in the south. Thomas Jefferson planted pomegranates at Monticello in 1771. Meanwhile, the Spanish introduced pomegranates to their colonies in the New World and in 1769 Spanish settlers brought them to California, where they flourished.

The Mediterranean climate of Marin County is ideal for pomegranates. Grown either as small trees (from twelve to twenty feet high) or shrubs, the rose-like flowers called balaustines and uniquely shaped fruit make them suitable for use as ornamental specimens in the garden. Their leathery, lance-shaped leaves may drop in winter or remain throughout the year. Dwarf pomegranates are popular bonsai plants because of their attractive flowers and unusual red-brown bark that becomes gray and twisted with age. They are also well-suited for use as container plants.

Pomegranates prefer a warm, sunny location and well-drained soil, but will do well even in rock-strewn gravel. They will also grow in partial shade. Cultivation instructions remain the same as those given by the English Quaker Peter Collison in a letter to the botanist John Bartram in Philadelphia in 1762: "Plant it against the side of thy house, nail it close to the wall. In this manner it thrives wonderfully with us, and flowers beautifully, and bears fruit this hot year. I have twenty-four on one tree."

To establish new plants, they should be watered every two to four weeks. Regular irrigation will improve fruit yield, however, once established, the trees or bushes can withstand drought.

Pomegranates will self-pollinate, but more fruit will set if they are cross-pollinated by insects. The fruit will mature five to seven months after bloom. Pick fruit as soon as it matures; over-mature fruit tends to split open, especially if rained on.

In the northern hemisphere, pomegranates fruit from September through January. The fruit may be stored for up to seven months between 32 degrees and 41 degrees F. (0 and 5 degrees C.)

A number of pomegranate cultivars have been developed in California, including Balegal, Cloud, Crab, Early

Wonderful, Fleshman, Granada, Green Globe, Home, King and Phoenicia. The cultivar Wonderful originated in Florida and was first propagated in California in 1896. Today it is the leading commercially cultivated pomegranate in California.

Some varieties have spines and others are spineless. In my own garden in Greece, I have a bush with spines and a tree without spines. I definitely prefer the spineless variety. In July, 2015, my pomegranate tree burned down in the large fire that devastated Voion. By the next spring, numerous shoots sprouted from the tree's base. I had the choice of maintaining it as a bush or developing it as a tree. I decided to leave only two of the strongest shoots. By repeatedly pruning off the lower branches, I have now created a small, double-trunked tree.

To serve a pomegranate, score the leathery skin vertically and break it open. Separating the red arils (seed casings) from the white pith and capillary membrane is easiest if done in a bowl of water. The arils will drop and the white membrane will float.

Eat the juice-encased seeds whole. They may be sprinkled on salads or used to decorate fish or vegetable dishes. Take care when eating pomegranates: the red juice will permanently stain fabric—in fact, it is used as a dye.

Pomegranate juice can be extracted by squeezing fruit halves on an orange juice squeezer. Pomegranate juice has been commercially available in the United States since 2002 and is becoming increasingly popular. It may be used in salad dressings, to marinate or glaze meat, or to flavor sauces. Pomegranate juice is the base for grenadine syrup. Pomegranate concentrate is used in many Syrian and Persian dishes. In modern Iran, the fruit is believed to give long and healthy life.

In 2020, for the first time since the fire, I am once again enjoying home-grown pomegranates: Yeia mas—To our health!

## *Cultivating Fig Trees*

~

August is the month to savor succulent figs. Growing up in Colorado, I had eaten only dried figs. In California, I learned to love fresh figs. Several varieties of this fragile fruit are available at farmers' markets and in grocery stores. But the best fruits are those picked from the fig tree in one's own garden.

Figs have been enjoyed for thousands of years—since at least 5,000 B.C.E., based on archeological excavations. Traditionally, figs are a symbol for peace and security in life: "[and they] dwelt in safety...every man under his vine and his fig tree." (1 Kings 4:25)

There are over nine hundred species of *Ficus*. They originated in tropical and subtropical areas of Asia and were distributed by man throughout the Mediterranean Basin. From there, fig shoots were carried to the New World. Six varieties are especially well-suited to cultivation in California: Golden, primarily eaten as dried fruit; Mission, eaten both dried and fresh; and Brown Turkey, Kadota, Sierra, and Tiger, all eaten fresh.

Figs thrive in Mediterranean climates, such as we enjoy in the Bay Area, with a high number of sunny days, light winds and low average rainfall; they grow well at elevations up to 3,000 feet (900 meters). There are some hardy cultivars that can be grown in the high desert and in the Northwest, even in Canada. The ideal location offers full sun, a southern exposure, and protection from prevailing winds and late frosts. A brick or stone wall will provide protection as well as reflected warmth.

I recently planted a fig tree in a small garden area. My intention was to eventually enjoy the delicious fruit and provide a living screen. Immediately, a neighbor stuck her head out the window and told me that I had chosen a terrible place to plant a fig. "Why is that?" I asked. "Because they are so messy," she replied, "They drop their leaves and all that squishy fruit." "What would you suggest for this spot then?" I inquired. "Viburnum," came her quick response.

I was not immediately convinced. I had visions of eating tree-ripened figs: the spring breba crop, born on last season's growth, and the fall main crop, born on new growth. I like the look of fig trees. The twisted branches and large, lobed leaves appeal to me. And when fig trees are pruned, they can develop into broad bushes. It could even be espaliered to cover the wrought iron railing.

A few days later another Greek neighbor offered her wisdom on the subject. "See that big fig tree behind my house?" she asked. I gazed at the venerable old tree, probably forty feet high and at least as wide. "Fig trees seek water, you know. That fig tree's roots grew right through the wall into our laundry room. Then they grew around a water pipe and squeezed it so hard, it broke. My father had to replace the pipe."

Oh dear, I thought. Maybe I should move that little tree.

Belatedly, I remembered what I have often recommended to other gardeners: When choosing a location for a tree, do some basic research regarding the ultimate size of the tree and site it accordingly. I should follow my own advice. Thus, I have decided to plant my fig tree in the sunny corner of a large garden area, away from the house, where it can grow to its full and glorious size.

~ *Fruits of the Garden* ~

Fig trees are generally very tough plants, requiring little water and little maintenance once established. Planted in an appropriate spot, they can be attractive and productive additions to the garden.

They may be attacked by some pests, but these can be controlled. To stymie gophers, who love to eat fig roots, I could plant the tree in a large aviary wire basket. Happily, deer don't like to eat figs. Birds, however, will damage the fruit. Other potential pests include botrytis and fig canker. Botrytis is generally not fatal and will stop in the spring. To prevent it, I would carefully remove all damaged fruit and fruit mummies. Fig canker usually starts at sunburned areas of the branches or trunk and can be prevented by whitewashing.

I am not giving up my dream of picking sun-warmed, ripe figs from the tree and popping them directly into my mouth. It will take my fig tree several years to start producing fruit.

In the meantime, friends have brought me figs from their own trees to prepare a warm fig salad: I halve the figs and place them, cut side up, in the oven at a low heat until they are warmed through; toss mixed greens with balsamic dressing (three quarters of a cup of olive oil whisked into one tablespoon of Dijon mustard and one quarter cup of balsamic vinegar); and serve the warmed fig halves on a bed of mixed greens, interspersed with chunks of fresh goat cheese. Sitting on my balcony, ourselves warmed by the afternoon sun, we enjoy the quintessential flavors of the Mediterranean.

# Growing and Preparing Table Olives

~

The Mediterranean climate of Marin County is ideal for cultivating olive trees. A number of commercial olive farms have taken root in our county. But any household garden may have enough room for one olive tree—and that is all you need. The commercial growers cultivate trees that produce olives for oil. The backyard gardener wants to produce olives for the table.

Several years ago, growing olive trees seemed mysterious to me. Now I have been overseeing my own olive farm in Greece with one hundred trees for twelve years and growing olive trees seems much simpler. On my farm, sixty trees are Koroneiki, small trees that produce small olives with relatively large pits, unsuitable for the table but producing high-quality oil. Thirty-eight trees are Athenas, large trees that produce medium-sized olives suitable for either oil or the table. I have two trees that produce olives specifically for the table: one Kalamata and one Chalkidiki, also called Gaidero or "donkey olive." Kalamata olives are large black olives generally preserved so they remain rather salty. Gaideros are giant green olives, often served stuffed with garlic or almonds or blue cheese. My advice to the backyard gardener would be to choose one of these two varieties or, if your yard is large enough, one of each.

Olive trees are extremely hardy. They do not require additional water once established. Olive trees naturally produce large crops one year and minimum crops the next. However, by watering your olive trees during the dry sum-

*~ Fruits of the Garden~*

mer season, you can encourage them to produce large crops each year. Even young trees produce some olives. It is thrilling to eat olives from your own tree, even one jarful.

Olive trees should be fertilized once a year in January. If you want to produce a maximum yield every year, you can fertilize your trees more often. My olive farm is certified organic by one of the European Union certification organizations. Thus, I use only organic fertilizer on my trees.

Olives are susceptible to the Mediterranean fruit fly. Unfortunately, this pest lives in Marin County as well as in the Mediterranean. The flies lay an egg under the skin of the developing olive and as the hatched maggot grows, it eats the olive. If a fly does lay an egg in an olive, you can see a mark at the entrance hole. Those olives must be discarded, as they are not fit for the table.

Many commercial olive growers protect their trees against attack by the fruit flies by spraying with a pesticide, because the infected olives raise the acidity level of the oil. The best quality olive oil has a low acidity level, indicating minimal impurities in the oil. On my organic farm, I do not spray with pesticides, therefore more of my olives may be damaged by fruit flies—and more of my table olives discarded.

Processing olives for the table is a labor-intensive job: table olives must be picked by hand. Then before they are put into salt water to preserve them, they must be sorted through to eliminate fly-infested or otherwise damaged fruit. Giant Gaidero olives may be slit on three sides with a paring knife, so the brine will penetrate the olives. Kalamatas may also be slit if you desire, but it's not imperative. Put the olives in a large jar and fill the jar with water. Raw olives are extremely bitter and inedible. To leech the bitterness out of olives, change the water every twenty-four hours until the olives are no longer bitter. Then place the olives in saltwater. The level of salt in the water is easy to determine: float a raw egg in its shell in the salt water. You have added enough salt when about one-third of the egg is above water. Remove the egg.

The olives can remain in salt water until you decide to eat them, up to a year or more. When you do decide to eat them, there are many different ways to prepare them. But first you need to taste one. If it is too salty, you can leech out the salt by putting the olive in fresh water overnight. Taste another one. If still too salty, change the water and taste one the next day.

Once the olives have a nice flavor, rinse them in fresh water and cover them in olive oil. You may add some red wine vinegar to the oil to sharpen the flavor. Or add slivers of garlic to the oil. The olives will be infused with garlic flavor. Try adding hot peppers to create spicy olives. Olives—either in brine or in oil—do not need to be refrigerated. If you do refrigerate them, the oil solidifies and will need to return to room temperature before you can eat the olives.

Prepared olives can be eaten as appetizers, added to salads, used to flavor baked dishes or stews. The savory fruit is a healthful addition to any meal. Even a single tree may provide a tasty and satisfying harvest.

# Jujube Dates

~

When I think of dates, I think of date palms in the desert. However, the red dates, black dates and honey dates found in local Oriental markets are not the fruit of palms, but of jujube trees, *Ziziphus jujuba*. With their deep roots, jujube trees tolerate desert conditions and are worthy of consideration for drought-tolerant gardens. Jujubes also tolerate saline and alkaline soils, although they will produce more fruit and thrive in richer loam. They are resistant to insect pests and disease. Deciduous trees with a graceful, gnarled form, they generally grow from twelve to fifteen feet tall.

Sources differ as to the origins of the tree—some say Syria, others claim China. Regardless of their point of origin, jujubes are now grown in northern Africa, southern Europe, Russia, India, through the south and west of the United States and as far north as Pennsylvania and Oregon, as well as in the Middle East and China.

Jujube fruit ripens in late summer to early fall and resembles small apples. The skin is pale green that becomes mottled with red as the fruit matures. It has a crisp texture and sweet flavor. After ripening, the fruit may be left on the tree, where it will dry and become red dates. The dried fruit will last indefinitely—no preservation required.

According to traditional Chinese herbal medicine, red dates, or *hong zao*, clear the nose, throat, and sinuses. In Britain, jujube was used as a remedy for sore throats and coughs. Lozenges that included the fruit were called jujubes (JOO-joo-bees), and the name came to refer to any lozenge or soft sweet. The correct pronunciation of the fruit is "joo-JOO-bee" according to Roger Meyer, who grows jujubes commercially in Valley Center, California.

There are 400 varieties of jujubes. 'Li' and 'Land' are the two most commonly available cultivars. They were originally introduced to California by Frank Meyer of Meyer lemon fame. He imported improved Chinese varieties to the Plant Introduction Station at Chico, California in the early 1900s.

'Li' has large, round fruit that grow up to three ounces in mid-August. The tree is many-branched, yet narrow and upright. The fruits are best eaten fresh. Sources recommend this as the best first jujube tree to have.

'Lang' has large, pear-shaped fruit that should be allowed to achieve full red color before eating. This fruit is one of the best to let dry on the tree.

'So,' a somewhat dwarfed tree, grows in a zig-zag branching pattern. At each stem node, new growth takes off at ninety degrees. Its shape is most striking in wintertime. It fruits mid-season.

'Topeka,' from eastern Kansas, has excellent, late-season fruit.

Although eating and cooking with jujube has not caught on yet in the United States, in parts of the world jujube is an important fruit crop. In Jodhpur, India, the Central Arid Zone Research Institute has carried out a thirty-year research and development program and selected fifty cultivars for commercial development as a perennial fruit tree crop for arid lands. In India, 90,000 hectares of land (about 225,000 acres) and 300,000 people are engaged in jujube cultivation. For commercial cultivation, high productivity and the ability to be transported and stored are key factors. In China, the largest producer, dried jujube dates are used to flavor soups and salty dishes. In traditional Chinese medicine, uses extend well beyond that of a cold remedy.

In home gardens, a jujube tree can provide not only an attractive focal point, but also contribute to a habitat attractive to birds, that will compete with the gardener for the fruit. Edward Hagar sums up the attractions of jujubes: "Gardeners who visit my backyard garden-orchard in Thousand Oaks, California, usually ask why I have so many jujube trees. My answer is easy: no other tree gives me so much pleasure for so little effort."

# Not-so-tropical Guava

~

When we bought our house just before Thanksgiving, there were guava fruits on the three small trees in our lower yard. I had not seen any fruits again until this fall, when I tripped over one.

At first, I didn't recognize the smooth four-inch oval green fruit with dried sepals protruding from one end. Then I looked up the slope at the bush-like guavas and saw two dozen more. Always delighted with any produce from my garden, I gathered them up and took them to the kitchen. Although I had purchased guava jelly in Hawaii and enjoyed drinking guava juice in the tropics, I wasn't quite sure what to do with my bounty.

Guava is native to the Americas, from Mexico to Peru. It may have been domesticated in Peru several thousand years ago. In archaeological sites there, guava seeds have been found stored with seeds of other cultivated plants. Commercial cultivation of guava in the Caribbean islands was first reported by Europeans in 1526.

Early explorers carried guava seeds to Asia, Africa, India and the Pacific islands. Today guava is grown throughout the world's tropical and sub-tropical regions.

Guava trees generally grow from eight to twenty feet tall and may look more like shrubs than trees. They thrive at elevations from sea level to 3,000 feet (900 meters) and tolerate a wide range of soil conditions. Plants grown in well-composted soil will be healthier and produce more fruit. Fruit production is also reputedly heavier following a cool winter season. The plants are drought- and neglect-tolerant. However, they suffer damage at temperatures much below freezing.

In California, they grow from the southern border as far north as Mendocino County. Small varieties are suitable for container gardening and can be moved inside in harsh weather.

Guava is a medicinal herb. In various parts of the world, a tea made from the leaves and bark is used as an astringent and bactericide, and as a remedy for diarrhea, dysentery and other gastrointestinal disorders. Its vitamin C content is higher than citrus.

There are several species of guava. The subtropical species we see in the San Francisco Bay area is *Psidium cattleianum*. Here we have both strawberry guava (*P. cattleianum Sabine*) and lemon guava (*P. cattleianum ssp. lucidum Degener*). Both these varieties can be grown anywhere citrus succeeds. Tropical guava (*P. guajava*) grows throughout the tropics, yields soft, juicy fruit, and may reach forty feet in height. Brazilian guava (*P. guineense*) is an evergreen shrub with fruit described as small, yellow and too bitter to be palatable. Depending on the variety, the fruit may be round, ovoid or pear-shaped. The skin may be thick or thin. Seeds may be soft or rock-hard, as in varieties grown for juice. The pulp ranges from cream-colored to bright pink.

Here is what I did with my lemon guavas: The simplest way to prepare the fruit is akin to making applesauce. Wash the fruit, cut off the ends, and quarter lengthwise. No need to peel them or remove the seeds. Add some water and a bit of ground cinnamon, and simmer over a very low heat until the guavas turn to mush. Add brown sugar, if necessary, and puree with a hand blender. The sauce can be served over ice cream.

I decided to whip some cream into stiff peaks and fold in the cooled guava puree. Instant guava mousse! Guava fruits contain pectin, which works almost like gelatin to firm the dessert.

Having enjoyed the harvest so much this year, I plan to pay more attention to my guava trees. Soon I will put compost around the base of the trees and prune them, removing water shoots and suckers. Fruit is borne on new growth, and I hope to increase next year's yield.

# Growing Grapes

~

Since ancient times, grape arbors have graced gardens and supported vines producing grapes for the table and for wine production. The oldest known wine jar dates from between 5400 and 5000 B.C.E. in the Neolithic Period. The Egyptians created a hieroglyph representing a grape arbor. Symbolic of peace and security, the Bible says, "They will sit under their grapevines and their fig trees, and no one will be afraid." (Micah 4:4)

In the Mediterranean climate of Marin County, grape vines thrive. Grapes prefer well-drained soil and will require moderate summer watering until well-established.

In the wild, grape vines sprawl along the ground or clamber over rocks or dead trees. But to protect the fruit as it develops, cultivated vines are generally supported either on trellises or on arbors. As well as providing support for grapevines, garden arbors can provide a focal point for the garden, creating inviting spaces of dappled shade.

Arbors may take many forms. Arches create a sense of anticipation, the feeling that something interesting must be happening on the other side. Rectangular arbors may shelter a location for a picnic table or outdoor seating. Arbors may cover a walkway, leading from one section of the garden to another. Or they may be asymmetrical in shape, perhaps in the form of a half circle creating a backdrop for open space.

In order to support the weight of one or more vines, grape arbors must be very sturdily built. The poles supporting the arbor should be set in cement with at least six inches of gravel underneath the posts to allow for drainage. A vine can be planted at each post, although one vine will eventually grow large enough to cover even a large arbor.

According to farm adviser Paul Vossen, "Grapes, *Vitis* species, are an ideal crop plant for mild climactic areas of California. The unique coastal climate allows the production of some of the world's highest-quality wine grapes and, consequently, some of the world's best wines. Table grapes do very well in almost all of California, excluding the very cold mountain areas. Table fruit should be grown so that the clusters are shaded by the leaves of the vine while wine grapes generally need some sun exposure to the clusters starting just after bloom."

There are several thousand varieties of grapes from which to choose, but there are a few outstanding varieties that the home gardener should consider. If you are planning to produce your own wine, you may decide to plant early-maturing chardonnay, sauvignon blanc, cabernet franc or pinot noir, or late-maturing semillon, white Riesling, cabernet sauvignon or merlot.

Table grapes are of either European or American origin. European varieties include Thompson seedless, tokay and muscat of Alexandria. American table grape varieties include perlette, flame seedless and red globe.

Perhaps the most traditional American table grape is Concord, which can be used for jellies and grape juice as well. In her article, "How to Build Concord Grape Arbors," Gail Cohen writes, "Discovered growing wild in Concord, Mass., in the late nineteenth century, this indigenous grape variety quickly became a favorite of farmers who marveled at the fruit's ability to withstand harsh weather conditions.

Early harvests don't diminish the juicy taste of Concord grapes, and if you're in it for the long haul, you'll be pleased to learn that while grapes take around three years to mature, the well-tended arbor will give you up to forty years' worth of sweet crops."

On my olive farm in Greece, the previous owner planted a row of grape vines. He supported them on wire strung between pieces of rebar hammered into the ground. As an alternative to the trellis style, I have tried to prune these vines into the ancient "gobelet" shape. Romans pruned their vineyards this way. Today, some vintners select it for varietals like Grenache and Mourvedre that have strong wood and an upright growth pattern. The objective is to create an open structure with four arms around a central base. With a few vines, I have succeeded. My other vines must be varieties like Syrah, whose branches are too weak to stand upright and therefore trail along the ground. I allow these vines to drape over the stone terrace wall and hang down towards the raised bed below.

For me, the value of my grape vines is aesthetic. I love the way they look. Rather than compete with birds and insects for the fruit, I leave it on the plants as part of the natural wildlife habitat.

# Mushrooms for the Garden

~

One overcast Saturday, I spent the afternoon at the Presidio Community Garden learning how to grow edible mushrooms. This is different than seeking and trying to identify various species of wild mushrooms that grow in my garden. Whereas wild mushrooms are fascinating to pick and match with photos and descriptions—in order to determine whether they are edible, "pukey poisonous" or downright deadly—growing mushrooms is as intentional as planting a rose.

Ken Litchfield of the Mycological Society of San Francisco (MSSF) gave us a thorough grounding in mushroom cultivation. He explained that the mushrooms we eat are the fruit of the mushroom "plant." Mushrooms, species of fungus, used to be classified taxonomically as plants, but fungi are now a separate kingdom. The fungus "plant" itself is the whitish web of mycelium that threads its way through a substrate such as decomposing leaves, wood chips, sawdust, hay, or compost. Since the fungus is underground, we don't see it. When conditions are right, the mycelium produces its "fruit"—that is, the mushroom that contains the spores from which new mycelium could grow. We can harvest mushrooms from our gardens just as we harvest tomatoes or beans.

Mushroom mycelium can be purchased from various sources either locally or online. Mushrooms can also be grown from cuttings.

*~ Fruits of the Garden ~*

Just as one prepares soil for garden plants, the gardener must prepare the substrate for mushrooms. At the Presidio Community Garden, Litchfield had us spread finely ground, wet wood chips about nine inches deep in a shady bed. Fresh hardwood chips are best. They may be obtained from a tree cutting company. Eucalyptus and softwood evergreens, such as pine, spruce, fir and cedar, contain chemicals that only certain mushrooms can tolerate. Hay, leaves, humus or compost may also be used as substrate. Check to see what type of substrate the mushroom you are planting prefers. Litchfield then gave us chunks of mycelium that we buried in the woodchips and watered thoroughly. The mycelium will grow through the woodchips, extracting the nutrients it requires as it decays the wood.

Mushrooms can be grown in wood chips or other substrate in planter boxes or containers. It is critical to keep the containers shaded and damp, as they will dry out faster than substrate on the ground.

Mushrooms can be grown inside. At the annual MSSF Fungus Fair, I purchased a tree-oyster mini-farm: a block of substrate grown through with mycelium. I put it in my utility room, slit its plastic bag as directed and misted it with water a couple of times each day. The first flush of mushrooms has already delicately flavored scrambled eggs, risotto and other dishes. After I have harvested the second or third flush, I will break up the block of substrate and plant it in my garden.

Mushrooms may also be planted in freshly cut logs. This method uses inch-long, one-fourth-inch-diameter wooden dowels that have been coated with mycelium of a wood-eating species. To plant, drill holes several inches deep in the log, squirt in some water, and push three or four dowels into the holes. To keep the moisture in, plug the end of the hole with wax. This is a project for a patient gardener. It takes a year or two for the log to become fully infiltrated by mycelium. Only then will the mycelium begin to fruit. The log should continue to bear mushrooms for two to four more years. During our Saturday afternoon seminar, we took turns drilling holes and plugging them with dowels. I liked the idea, but I need more immediate results.

According to Litchfield, one can grow mushrooms from cuttings from either grocery store or wild mushrooms. Layer mushroom bases, with or without attached mycelium, between pieces of damp, unwaxed cardboard. Place the layers in a closed plastic bag to keep them damp until the mycelium has grown throughout the substrate. Then the layers can be planted in additional substrate in the garden. If the cuttings were taken from wild mushrooms, try to duplicate the conditions where they were picked.

In addition to oyster mushrooms, garden giant, coral mushrooms, blewits, shaggy manes and giant morels are popular species for cultivation.

Litchfield's excellent seminar and the pleasure I have derived from my mushroom mini-farm have convinced me of the value of cultivating mushrooms in my garden. I know a shady spot that will be greatly improved by a deep cover of woodchips—and the mushroom mycelium that will silently develop there until we can enjoy its mushroom fruit.

# *Considering Food as Medicine*
### ~

According to Western tradition, "you are what you eat." Chinese tradition takes this concept even further, examining foods and classifying their properties by their effect on the human body.

Yin foods are those believed to promote cooling in the body; yang foods promote warming. Ideally, one achieves a physical balance of yin and yang. When someone becomes ill, the belief goes, it is because that balance has been disturbed.

Chinese traditional medicine strives to restore balance through a combination of medicinal foods and herbs. In fact, there is no firm distinction between food and medicine. When I first became interested in Chinese medicinal foods and herbs, I assumed they must all be unusual and exotic plants. I quickly learned I am growing a number of them in my own garden: I just wasn't aware of it. As I learn more about the nature of the fruits and vegetables I cultivate, I become more aware of my own diet and think more about how to promote my family's health through what we eat every day.

For example, I have an apple tree in my garden. According to Chinese tradition, apple is cool (yin) and acts on the lungs, stomach and large intestine. Its healing effects include improving appetite and digestion, lowering blood sugar and relieving alcohol intoxication.

Also in my yard is an apricot tree, though it has not been bearing much fruit the last couple of years, and the fruit that does appear is often damaged by birds and squirrels. Apricots are considered neutral (neither yin nor yang) and good for relieving dry cough, sore throat and constipation.

We also have a large female kiwi vine. For it to bear fruit, a male kiwi vine must be growing nearby. The male vines I have planted have proved to be much less hardy than the female; the second male died last year. Kiwi fruit is considered cool (yin), acting on the kidney, liver and stomach, and helpful against kidney and urinary stones.

In the past, I have used the fruit from my guava bushes as a dessert, boiled with a little brown sugar, pureed and mixed with whipped cream for an instant tropical mousse. Now I know that guava is considered warm (yang) and is used as a Chinese medicinal food to stop diarrhea and bleeding.

The list of vegetables considered medicinal foods includes cauliflower, cucumber, lettuce, potato, tomato, zucchini, bok choy, mustards, snow peas, yard-long beans and many kinds of melon. Here is specific information about some others:

Green onions are considered to be warm (yang) and helpful in warming the body, inducing perspiration, healing swelling and relieving nasal discharge associated with the common cold.

Asparagus, the vegetable that signals spring to me, is considered slightly warm (yang) and helpful in relieving coughs, lowering blood pressure, expanding terminal blood vessels and relieving swelling.

Eggplant is considered a cool (yin) food that relieves coughs and pain, prevents hardening of blood vessels and treats atherosclerosis.

Western medical tradition often uses one medicine at a time to promote healing. By contrast, Chinese traditional medicine used combinations of medicinal foods and herbs—often twelve to fifteen together—for a desired effect.

Mixing foods and herbs with similar properties increases the overall effectiveness. Mixing herbs and foods with different properties can moderate the effects of the main herbs and minimize adverse side effects.

The Chinese call foods that have few or no adverse side effects and that can be used as tonics over a long period of time "superior herbs." Garlic is a superior herb, used to protect against parasites, fungi and toxins, as an anti-inflammatory and to protect against heart disease. Another superior herb is mandarin orange peel, dried in the sun and aged by storing it dry. The older the peel is, the more effective its medicinal effect is reputed to be. It is used to relieve nausea and vomiting, abdominal swelling and local infection.

Here in the San Francisco Bay area there is a wealth of information about Chinese medicinal herbs and foods. Quarryhill Botanical Garden, near Glen Ellen in Sonoma County, houses one of the largest collections of scientifically documented, wild source, temperate Asian plants in North America. Peg Schafer, owner of the Chinese Medicinal Herb Farm in Petaluma, is a nationally renowned expert in the traditional and contemporary cultivation and use of Chinese herbs. The Farm maintains a collection of over three hundred species of medicinal plant species.

Considering foods as medicine is a new way of thinking for me. It does make sense that whatever I eat has some effect on my body's well-being. To understand the medicinal effects of all the foods I eat means I have a tremendous amount to learn.

~

CHAPTER SIX

~

*Garden Design*

## *Aromatic Entryways*

~

In Greece, it is customary to place a pot of basil near the front door so guests may brush their hands against it and savor the fragrance before entering the house. Aromatic entryway gardens create a welcoming atmosphere. The visual attraction of the garden is enhanced by the scent of the herbs, warmed by the sun.

In two gardens I have created in Greece, I extended the principle to include perennial aromatic herbs: rosemary, lavender, oregano and lemon verbena.

Two varieties of lavender grace the garden in the front terrace garden. One has grayish leaves and medium-length flower spikes. It threatens to take over the narrow, raised bed. Regular pruning keeps it within bounds without dampening its enthusiastic presence.

The second lavender has pale green leaves and is a more restrained presence. Its fragrance is not quite as intense as the gray-leaved lavender, though clearly recognizable. Its flower spikes are not long, integrating the blooms into its branches.

I planted two *Rosmarinus officinalis* 'Prostratus' in the bed, one near the edge, hoping that its branches would eventually trail over the side of the bed. It has taken several years for that to happen, but some of its branches now reach the ground. The other rosemary is near the wall. Its looping branches give the effect of a piece of sculpture in the background.

Hiding behind the rosemary is a single lemon verbena. It unfortunately has not flourished in this environment, but even a single leaf, rubbed between the fingers, emits a strong fragrance. A few leaves steeped in boiling water produce a savory tea.

In the forefront of the bed, an oregano plant produces more than enough small, round leaves to flavor all kinds of dishes. It, too, requires pruning, and the dried leaves will last all winter long.

In back of the gray lavender, I have attempted to espalier a bougainvillea. Its dark red blooms (modified leaves rather than true flowers; the flowers are tiny cream-colored forms that look almost like stamens) make a strong contrast against the whitewashed garden wall.

On my olive farm, I built an entryway garden bed of stone. It is an entryway to a large patio along the footpath to my house, and the concept is the same. The fragrance of the plants sends a clear message: "Welcome to this place."

Here the lemon verbena is much happier and is developing into a round, bushy form. I also planted two gray-leaved lavenders and one oregano, which is still struggling, establishing itself. The fuschia-colored bougainvillea will eventually cover much of the stone terrace behind the garden bed. Two prostrate rosemary plants are beginning to crawl and sprawl their way to the boundaries of the bed.

Another fragrant plant that welcomes visitors is the rose-scented geranium, officially known as *Pelargonium graveolens*. A single plant has grown to gigantic proportions, escaping its small bed and cascading down between two houses. Its leaves have a distinctive fragrance and are used to flavor desserts and jelly, as well as iced drinks. And, as some French friends told me, the fragrant leaves—which they call *citronelle*—help keep away mosquitoes: good reason to plant it near a seating area.

*~ Garden Design ~*

All these plants are native to the Mediterranean region, and thus also thrive in the Marin County climate. Once established, they require very little summer water. Mediterranean plants are naturally dormant during the summer months, when there is little, if any, rain. They grow and flower in the winter and spring. The fragrance—and flavor—of their leaves becomes more intense the drier they are. During the hottest days of August this summer, I decided to take pity on my garden plants and water them. Immediately, they all responded with new leaves and the lavenders sent out new buds. I'm not sure I did the plants any favor, however. There is good reason for their growth cycle: plants need some time to rest.

In a Mediterranean climate, the Mediterranean natives described above will require only a minimum of water during summer months, making them a perfect addition to a Marin garden, and a welcoming, aromatic addition to any entryway.

# Green Roofs and Living Walls

~

Perhaps the idea originated with the Hanging Gardens of Babylon of 600 B.C.E., renowned for gardens that trailed down from terraces. In the sixteenth century, the ivy-covered walls of European manor houses continued the practice. The green sod roofs on nineteenth-century frontier prairie dwellings may have been more necessity than choice. History informs us that green roofs and living walls have been around for thousands of years. With current interest in sustainable landscaping practices, these historic techniques are attracting new attention.

According to one definition, sustainable landscaping "comprises numerous practices that address environmental issues related to the design, construction, implementation, and management of residential and commercial landscapes." The environmental issues sustainable landscaping addresses include global climate change, air pollution, water pollution, water shortages and drought, storm water management, pesticide toxicity, soil health, fertilizer runoff, non-renewable resources and energy usage.

Green roofs and living walls address a number of these issues. They can:

- reduce the heat produced by urban environments;
- improve air quality due to the filtering mechanism of the plants and substrate;

- decrease the waste of water, for example water running off a green roof can be used inside the house for flushing toilets;
- significantly reduce the surface runoff of rainfall, thus reducing storm water management requirements;
- reduce the need for air conditioning and provide a degree of insulation in winter;
- provide sound insulation from the combined effects of soil, plants and trapped layers of air.

Additionally, green roofs and living walls can provide habitat for insects and birds and provide efficient green space for recreation and for growing flowers and vegetables.

**Green Roofs**

As American pioneers knew, green roofs provide insulation, allowing houses to remain relatively cool in summer's heat, although sod roofs were notoriously leaky and dirt could filter through cloth ceilings. Today's green roofs provide similar insulation benefits, but protect the building with an impervious waterproof layer, covered with several different layers of substrate, topped with plants that are able to withstand harsh conditions. One of today's most popular green roof plants is sedum, a succulent that can tolerate long periods without rainfall. Using several different varieties of sedum, one may create colorful patterns. One landscaping company suggests that a company's logo can be planted into their roof, providing perennial advertising! Grasses, wildflowers and any number of—preferably native—plants may be employed.

Plants and substrate are heavy and this is a major consideration in determining whether or not an existing building can support a green roof. The pitch of the roof is not: landscapers plant green roofs on pitched roofs as well as flat roofs, carefully anchoring the substrate at intervals on a pitched roof. The initial cost of a green roof is higher than that of other roofing materials. However, annual maintenance costs can be relatively low. Because a green roof protects the waterproofing membrane on the roof from the elements and ultra-violet light, the life expectancy of the membrane may be doubled or tripled, thus reducing the overall cost of the installation.

**Living Walls**

The most basic living wall is a vine, planted in the ground next to a building, which climbs up the wall, clinging with its own tendrils: ivy is the best-known example. Ivy leaves may turn red in the fall, adding additional charm. However, the tenacious tendrils may loosen shingles. Ivy should be trimmed back or torn down periodically to keep it from becoming an attractive dwelling place for rats and other small animals.

Living walls may also be created by plants planted above the wall that grow downwards, for example "climbing" roses cascading down a staircase.

Living walls may be interior as well as exterior. Years ago, I cultivated Swedish ivy in a row of planters placed along a shelf high on a living room wall. The Swedish ivy eventually hung all the way to the floor—nine feet below the planters. The room was filled with natural light, indirectly available to the Swedish ivy. The plant-hung wall was the most striking feature of the room. I appreciated its beauty, but I was unaware of the health benefits to my family: increased oxygen due to the natural process of photosynthesis and increased humidity due to transpiration.

*~ Garden Design ~*

Today's living walls may take the form of planters on the ground or suspended on the sides of a building, with steel cables or mesh attached to the wall to support the plants. They can be next to building walls, providing insulation and protection for the wall surfaces—from the elements as well as from graffiti, or at a distance from them, providing a green screen against unattractive construction. Commercially available planters feature angled containers for individual plants that, as the plants mature, create massed walls of foliage. These planters may be used outside or inside. Interior designers incorporate living walls into residential and commercial décor because of plants' various colors and textures, as well as their calming, serenity-inducing effects.

The ancient Babylonians appreciated the value of being surrounded by plants—growing on roofs, hanging down walls. Today, with a focus on sustainable landscaping, we are rediscovering their wisdom.

# *Apartment Gardening*

*~*

Apartment gardening can be divided into indoors gardening, that is, inside the apartment, and outdoors gardening, outside on the balcony or in window boxes. Even if an apartment offers no possibility of gardening outdoors—no balcony and restrictions that do not allow window boxes—it is possible to enjoy the pleasures and benefits of cultivating plants.

In some ways, gardening indoors is easier than gardening outside: the temperature and other aspects of weather are controlled. Rain will not drench your plants, hail will not shred their leaves, wind will not tear off their branches. However, gardening indoors presents its own challenges.

Designing an apartment garden involves the same elements as designing any other garden. Consider the various sizes and shapes of plants your apartment can accommodate: horizontal, vertical, flat against the wall, hanging in a round shape, filling a corner, as a centerpiece in a bay window. As a design choice, in an apartment it is often better to choose a few plants that will add real presence to the apartment, rather than a number of small pots that may make an apartment seem cluttered and smaller than it already is.

First, consider the microclimates in your apartment. Which direction do your windows face? If your apartment faces north, your windowsills may provide prime locations for plants; however, if your windows face south, your windowsills may be too hot for plants to survive. Indirect light is sufficient, and may be preferable, for many plants. If your apartment has a dark space, choose a plant for that space that loves shade. However, all plants need light, so keep in mind that there are some locations that are too dark for any plant to survive. Even the most shade-tolerant plants require several hours of indirect light every day. The microclimate in the bathroom is typically moist, whereas the shelf over the radiator will be very dry in winter when the heat is on. Once you have determined what the microclimates in your apartment are, you can choose plants that will thrive in those environments.

Second, consider what spaces you have in your apartment for plants. Shelves are ideal places for plants. In a living room I once had, there was a shelf that ran the width of the room, just below the open-beamed ceiling. I placed a row of pots of Swedish ivy on the shelf. They received only indirect light, but the room was bright. The ivy loved that location. In time, the ivy plants cascaded all the way to the floor across the entire wall. We were living in a garden room.

Tables, bookcases and other furniture are not ideal locations for plants, because no matter how carefully you water your plants, there is always the possibility that the saucer underneath the plant may crack or overflow, and water will damage your table or ruin your books. Instead, consider a corner space for a vertical plant that can sit on a platform on the floor. *Ficus benjamina,* corn plants and curly-leafed palms are good choices.

The bathroom, with its moist environment, is the perfect place to hang a basket with maidenhair or asparagus fern.

The kitchen windowsill, or a shelf over the counter, offers an opportunity to grow a selection of herbs that will add fresh flavor to any dish you put together. I have tried to grow several species of herbs in one pot—basil, oregano, thyme and tarragon—and I cannot recommend it. The plants competed against each other for space and water: basil, thyme and tarragon suffered, and eventually oregano won. It's better to grow only one species in each pot and give each plant an opportunity to thrive in its own individual space.

Flowering plants will add color to your apartment. A pedestal table, the type used to hold an asparagus fern in Victorian times, can also be used for a vining geranium (*Pelargonium*) that will create a column of red or pink or white blossoms. Orchids are some of the most beautiful flowering plants to grow in an apartment. With proper care, they may rebloom year after year.

In the fall, paper white narcissus and hyacinth bulbs can be placed in vases with stones to hold them in place and watered regularly until they bloom. I force paper whites in a tall, clear glass vase to provide support for their long stems.

Plants require light, water and carbon dioxide to grow. All of these are available indoors. However, they must be provided in appropriate amounts. The greatest hazard apartment plants face is overwatering. It is very important to provide adequate drainage for plants in pots. Many decorative pots are not suitable for planting because they have no drainage holes in the bottom. Water accumulates in the bottom of these pots and eventually the roots of plants planted in them rot and the plants die.

To keep soil from leaking out of the bottom of pots with drainage holes, place a layer of gravel in the bottom of the pot or a product such as a fabric disk filled with pellets before adding potting soil.

Make sure the saucer under the pot is deep. When you water the plant, add water until water just begins to appear in the saucer, then stop. This means that you have added

*~ Garden Design ~*

enough water to reach all of the plant's roots. If the saucer is not deep enough, the water that flows through the soil will overflow the saucer.

Do not water the plant again until the water has disappeared from the saucer and the top half-inch of soil in the pot is dry. Liquid fertilizer can be added to water when watering, or fertilizer sticks can be added to the soil.

Provide the basic necessities for your plants, place them in locations where they will thrive, and enjoy the pleasures of apartment gardening.

# *Planting in Layers*

~

Gardens are works of art in progress: the process is never completed. Whether we are designing new sections of the garden, or making modifications as a garden matures, we have an opportunity to view the garden as a succession of layers. Layers can be either horizontal or vertical. In our three-dimensional garden spaces, we must consider both. In fact, as we make a choice in the horizontal dimension by filling a bed with plants, the vertical dimension is created by the heights of the plants we choose. As an artist layers in details to a drawing, we layer in plants of different sizes, colors and forms in our gardens.

The first layer to be considered in the garden is the hardscaping. Hardscaping is the walls, fences, paths, stairs, and patios around which the garden grows. The space between a sidewalk and fence offers the opportunity to plant a perennial border. Walls or fences offer opportunities for vertical plants, such as vines or climbing roses.

After the hardscaping, trees and bushes form the bones of the garden. They are the skeleton over which layers of annuals, perennials and vines will form the body.

In a formal garden, plants are often carefully spaced in even rows, according to height, from the shortest in the front to the tallest in the back of a given space. For example, a clipped boxwood hedge in front of medium-height geraniums in front of upright Tuscan rosemary. In a formal garden, plants farther from the center may be trimmed shorter, thus creating an optical illusion of distance and a much larger garden. Formal gardens, where plants are centered and each plant is balanced perfectly by a plant on either side, create a feeling of order and stability.

By contrast, most household gardens are informal. Groups or clumps of plants may be more pleasing than regular rows. Layering in this case may mean putting clumps of coreopsis in front of *Salvia greggii* and silvery-leaved Santolina. Groups of plants should be placed off-center to create a feeling of flowing movement. Layers of plants of different heights keep the eye moving throughout the garden.

Here are some examples of plants that can be used to create layers in the garden. A monochromatic color scheme can be created by using plants in different shades of one color, for example, purple. Low-growing lobelia could be used as the first layer, in front of Nepeta (catmint), in front of French lavender plants, in front of Mexican sage. Interspersing groups of white flowers, such as Erigeron (Santa Barbara daisy), will make colored flowers appear more brilliant.

When I first began planting my garden about ten years ago, I chose mostly medium-height plants. That made for a boring garden. Happily, over time, I began to fill in the edges with lower-growing plants and I added taller plants as a backdrop. Although I had read about the concept of layering in gardens, I didn't begin to really understand it until I discovered that the variety and interest created by layers were missing in my own.

In my garden, I use woolly thyme as a ground cover in front of a low-growing, dark purple verbena that grows beneath California poppies. Overshadowing the poppies, bronze daylilies grow in front of pink Valerian. Coyote bush and *Salvia clevelandii* are the anchoring bones.

Another aspect of layering is form. Gracefully arching leaves of daylilies contrast with the spear-like foliage of *Dietes* that bloom every two weeks or so, as their common name fortnight lilies implies. In one area of my garden, lavender and prostrate rosemary grow in front of a mature grevillea bush, and long stalks of salmon gladioli add colorful punctuation in between.

As my garden has matured and changed, I take the opportunity to add or replace plants with ones that add interest and complexity to my garden in layers of size and color and form.

# Coral Reef Inspiration

~

Once, I was snorkeling in an area called the Japanese Garden: a shallow reef in the Hollandes Cays of the San Blas Islands of Panama. As I swam slowly over the rich tapestry of hard and soft corals, I thought about why it might be called a garden and what it has in common with the gardens we create around our homes.

I realized that my vision of a garden had been too restricted, too homogeneous. The incredible variety of textures, forms, heights, colors and movement in this underwater garden was much more complex than anything I had imagined placing in juxtaposition in my own garden at home.

I began to think about Mediterranean garden plants that might perform the same functions in a domestic garden in Marin. Hard, domed coral heads, both reddish-brown and yellow, could be rocks in a garden landscape. Large rocks provide a sense of rest or repose when surrounded by the energy of growing plants. Slabs of yellow or red sandstone would create a different impression than boulders of chunky, gray granite.

Other corals were hard, but had many serrated edges. In a domestic garden, the equivalent effect could be created using horizontal evergreens such as junipers. The variations of color in the underwater aquatic garden were extremely beautiful. In the garden, yellow-tipped junipers can be used in conjunction with dark-green or bluish evergreens to enhance the color scheme.

Underwater, soft corals, some with a few arms and others with more complex branches, waft back and forth in the current. In a garden, grasses can perform this function as they move gently and gracefully in the breeze. Color and texture are of key importance: tall grasses such as bronze fountain grass will contrast with upright, straw-colored grasses or with rounded mounds of blue fescue.

Corals attain different heights and gardens can be thought of as growing in layers. Low, stiff-branched corals reminded me of perennial ground covers such as cotoneaster, or for color contrast, a low-growing maroon barberry. In the medium-height level, the garden might include prostrate rosemary or lavender. A taller level might include upright Tuscan rosemary or grevillea.

Bamboo is another plant that would fit into this amalgam of colors and textures, but in the garden it must be treated with care. Running varieties of bamboo can overtake an area; clumping varieties are more suitable for garden planting. Using a variety of heights, colors and textures, an entire garden could be planted with different species of bamboo.

In addition to the many shades of yellow, brown, bronze and rust of coral in the underwater garden, bright flashes of color are provided by tropical fish, such as yellow butterfly fish and blue and purple parrotfish.

In the above-ground garden, flowers provide these colorful accents. In traditional Japanese gardens, the majority of color is provided by the leaves of shrubs and trees, whether bronze, yellow or varying shades of green. Flowers are used to provide occasional bright flashes of pink, red, white or blue. Some of my favorite bright flowers are fuschia-colored bougainvillea, pink valerian and yellow daylilies. Easy annuals include pansies, petunias, marigolds and zinnias. The

*~ Garden Design ~*

possibilities of adding colorful flowers of any height, annual or perennial, to the garden are nearly endless.

The underwater coral garden was completely natural, unplanned by any garden designer. However, the colors, textures, different heights and forms all worked perfectly together.

Perhaps in my own garden planning, I have been too cautious, too wary of introducing contrasting colors and heights, different textures and shapes. I will undoubtedly proceed slowly, making gradual changes in my garden. But I will take into account the lessons I learned about gardening while snorkeling in the Japanese Garden in Panama.

# *Tranquility in a Japanese Garden*
~

Japanese gardens are some of the most tranquil spaces I know.

In studying them to determine how this effect is achieved, I have noted several common elements that may be incorporated into any garden design. These elements include pathways with scenic views, destinations, varied foliage with accents of color, stone lanterns or sculptures and water features.

A walk through a Japanese garden is a journey filled with discovery. Paths are curved so that each new direction offers a fresh vista, either of specific plants in the garden or a view beyond that is framed by trees. The path itself may be constructed of earth, wood or stone, but variations in the widths of steps or the size of paving stones will encourage the visitor either to keep moving or to stop and take an extra breath.

In a Japanese garden, there may be several destinations. When designing my garden using these principles, I placed a bench in a wide space at a split in the garden path. It is my favorite place for morning coffee. I can survey most of the lower part of the garden and watch birds and flying insects silhouetted against the filtered light. Another destination in my garden is a flat space dug into the hill between four oak trees. A gravel path leads to a Parisian café table and chairs. In a Japanese garden, this would be a wonderful spot for a teahouse. Seated at my table, I can see San Pablo Bay through oak branches. Ceanothus blooms lighten the hillside below me.

*~ Garden Design ~*

Japanese gardens rely largely on varied hues and textures of foliage to establish their tranquil atmosphere. Color is used as a seasonal accent. During spring, azaleas and rhododendrons burst into bloom, but during the rest of the year, the small leaves of the azaleas contrast with the large, oval leaves of the rhododendrons. Evergreens such as black pine and mugo pine and juniper provide another layer of contrast. Thin, arched leaves of lily turf, sword-like leaves of iris, and fronds of ferns add shape and texture to the overall design.

In one section of my garden, a Japanese stone lantern is surrounded by a black pine, a white azalea and rhododendrons of white, pink and red that bloom in succession. It is another destination. A simple bench against the wall of the house would create a perfect spot for meditation. Stone lanterns or sculptures provide focal points in the garden—and another reason to stop and reflect.

Water features in Japanese gardens may be as complex as waterfalls and streams, or as simple as a concave stone basin. Water is considered a purifying element, and in the absence of water, a stream of stones may achieve a similar effect.

Japanese gardens may be a few square meters in a courtyard outside a window, or many acres of winding paths, lakes and pavilions. The principles of creating serene spaces with peaceful views for rest and meditation are inherent to them all.

To learn more about Japanese gardens, I visited several public Japanese gardens in the Bay area. Hakone Japanese Garden in Saratoga is a fifteen-acre park with four sections: the Hill and Pond Garden, overlooking a pavilion; the Tea Garden; the Zen Garden, and the Bamboo Garden.

The Japanese Friendship Garden and Teahouse in San Jose is filled with symbols, such as irises symbolizing purity, innocence and chastity; a five-tiered pagoda, for the five elements of earth, wind, fire, water and metal; and a pond filled with koi, representing long life.

The San Mateo Japanese Garden is a small, enclosed garden with a path and bridges around a pond, a variety of stone lanterns, and the colored foliage of Japanese maples.

The Japanese Tea Garden and Tea House in San Francisco's Golden Gate Park was originally designed as a Japanese village for the 1894 Mid-Winter Exposition. It includes a dwarf conifer collection, in addition to paths, pools, small waterfalls and an arched bridge.

The University of California Botanical Garden in Berkeley includes a Japanese pool, surrounded by purple iris, pastel rhododendrons and lush green foliage.

In each of these Japanese gardens, paths with scenic views, destinations, varied foliage with accents of color, stone lanterns or sculptures and water features are used to create peaceful spaces offering a respite from the outside world. These are the elements I have used in my garden to create a sense of serenity.

# *A Rooftop Container Garden in Greece*

~

A friend with a house on the edge of the Mediterranean Sea in Greece asked me to design a container garden for her. Houses in Greece typically have flat roofs, and this neoclassical home in the crowded city of Piraeus had no garden space available other than the roof. In that sunny, warm climate, the roof can become an outdoor room, and this was my thought as I began considering the possibilities.

This would be a large garden room: about twenty-six by thirty feet. The house was sandwiched between higher buildings on the east and west sides. On the north side, a forty-inch high balcony wall contained the room. The inside wall was a new addition that had added two bedrooms and a bathroom to the original house. The addition had wood-framed windows and French doors and a gently sloping red-tiled roof that added a country feeling to the city garden. A black plastic tank containing fuel oil for heating was the single eyesore. A ledge extended along the sides of the neighboring buildings about thirty inches high and twelve inches wide.

My objective was to create a garden room requiring the least expense and minimum care. I thought about the color of flowers and foliage, the texture of leaves and needles. I also thought about form: plants growing up or down, wide or upright, horizontal and vertical lines, and what to put them in: round or rectangular shaped planters.

Wooden lattices with flowering vines growing on them would quickly create the sense of verdant walls and hide the neighboring buildings. The lattices I had installed reached from the ledge to the bottom of the tiled roof of the addition—about six feet high above the ledge, or eight and a half feet high total. On west side, I installed three pieces of lattice, each about five feet wide. On the east side, the wall was divided into two sections by a chimney. One section of lattices was six by ten feet, perfect for two pieces of lattice; the other section, five by six feet, held a piece of lattice placed horizontally.

Positioned on the ledge, at the base of each of the six pieces of lattice, I placed a rectangular planter with one purple-flowered potato vine (*Solanum*) in it. It was important to provide a large enough container with enough soil in it to support an eventually large, healthy vine.

In between each potato vine, also on the ledge, I placed another rectangular planter with one *Rosemarinus officinalis* 'Prostratus' in it. This species of rosemary tends to spread out flat, or if given the opportunity, down a wall. My intention was to have purple-flowered potato vines growing up and light-blue flowered prostrate rosemary growing down from the ledge. Again the planters each contained only one rosemary plant to provide enough soil for the plant to grow and thrive.

At the base of the balcony wall, I placed five pots, each with an oleander in it. These were large pots, twenty inches in diameter. The oleanders will eventually grow into a hedge that can be trimmed to a foot or so above the top of the balcony wall. Their pink and white blossoms will continue throughout the summer.

In the northwest corner, I placed two containers of photinia. The photinia's red foliage provides an elegant contrast to the green leaves of the vines and oleanders and the blue-gray needles of the rosemary. In front of the fuel tank, I placed one photinia, flanked by two dwarf lemon trees.

From the northeast corner of the balcony, you can see the sailboats and yachts in Pasalimani, the small harbor of Piraeus. To frame the view, I used two small olive trees whose branches will be trimmed into ball shapes. An upright rosemary and two pink azaleas fill the corner space without obstructing the view.

In the southwest corner, next to the window shutters, I put one more dwarf lemon tree. On the other side of the wooden shutters, I placed a small fir tree.

For a splash of bright color, in between each of the five oleanders, I placed a rectangular planter with two red geraniums. Next to the French door is an antique rectangular clay pot with butter-yellow daisy chrysanthemums.

To keep the plants well-watered throughout the hot summer months, I installed a drip irrigation system. The vines, shrubs and trees can all be served with one watering schedule: they all have low water requirements. The geraniums, azaleas and chrysanthemums will require some additional water each week.

The morning after the plants were installed, my friend said she spotted a butterfly. It was the first she has seen in Piraeus. More butterflies will surely follow.

# *Foiling Deer Gracefully*

~

Gentle, graceful deer emerge from the edge of the forest to graze in our hillside meadow. I harbor this image from years when I lived in Golden Gate Canyon in the foothills above Denver, Colorado. Here in Marin, deer emerge from the greenbelt to graze in my garden, which I do not appreciate at all. It took several years, during which the deer devoured dozens of newly-planted flowers and shrubs, before I began to understand the art of deer-resistant landscaping. I still make mistakes, but there are a number of plants that deer are not interested in eating. I have incorporated these in the deer-accessible section of the garden. The deer still roam through freely, but they inflict less damage.

When trying to determine whether or not a plant might be deer resistant, it helps to think like a hungry deer. Sharp, stickery plants scratch the throat. Long needles can get caught on the way down. Blade-like leaves are equally hard to swallow. Strong-smelling foliage, even though it might be the right texture, is off-putting. Plants that grow too close to the ground are hard to pull out, and if they have much of an odor, aren't worth the effort.

Plants that deer don't like to eat come in a variety of colors and shapes and range from trees to ground covers. Based on the categories of unappetizing plants described above, here are the plants in my garden that deer do not eat.

Sharp, stickery plants include asparagus fern and juniper. As anyone who has handled asparagus fern knows, those light, feathery fronds conceal sharp spines. Juniper is

*~ Garden Design ~*

an obvious throat-scratcher and I have a low-growing one spreading as a ground cover and another developing into a handsome specimen bush. Others in this category not in my own garden, but that I have observed growing unmolested nearby, are handsome magenta-leaved barberry and sprawling cotoneaster.

The long needles of my grevillea deter the deer. At this time of the year, it is covered with intricate pink and cream blossoms and appears especially graceful and delicate. My rosemary is filled with tiny blue flowers and will continue to bloom for months. The fragrant needles, so highly prized in cooking, hold no attraction for the deer.

Scattered throughout the garden are clumps of fortnight lilies, also called African iris. I prize them for their sword-like leaves, their upright form and their delicate blooms. They bloom once every two weeks, hence their name. The clumps may be divided easily and the new, smaller sections grow vigorously. Although their leaves are not as rigid as African iris, the bearded iris in my garden have likewise not been eaten by the deer.

Strong-smelling foliage is also of no interest to local deer. My Spanish lavender grows unmolested. I have read that some varieties of lavender are not deer-resistant and the other varieties of lavender I grow are in a deer-protected part of the garden. However, I can vouch for Spanish lavender. Its deep purple blooms are short-lived, but its gray-green foliage is attractive year-round. Santolina is another gray-leaved, deer-resistant plant. Soon it will be covered by tiny yellow blossoms that are lovely while they last. They are also an aggravation to deadhead, but the plant looks much better when I take the time to do it. Mint is an example of a fragrant plant deer do not eat. I let it run rampant in one corner of the garden and although I see deer prints in the soil, they leave the mint alone.

Three ground covers thrive despite the deer. Wooly thyme is fragrant and that may be the deterrent. Woodland strawberries are attractive to me, happily not at all to the deer. Similarly, *Vinca minor*, with its pale blue star flowers, is of no interest for grazing purposes. Another apparently delicate flower that deer do not eat is the vibrant orange California poppy. Paired with Spanish lavender, while it blooms for a few weeks in spring, it is stunning.

My calla lily, which has provided me with cut flowers for our entryway table for two months now, is completely unappealing to the deer. The plant will die back during the summer and the leaves will become limp and brown and mushy. At that point, I also find it unappealing. But the flowers bring me so much pleasure during their blooming season, I plan to divide it when it goes dormant this year and plant a few more clumps.

Shrubs the deer don't eat include heavenly bamboo (*Nandina*), oleander, Pride of Madeira (*Echium*), yew and rhododendron. Partially concealed by my white rhododendron is a large white azalea. The deer do not eat it, perhaps because it is a large shrub. I mistakenly thought this meant that azaleas in general were unattractive to deer. That is not the case in my garden. The new azaleas I planted were chewed voraciously by the deer, some to death. Belatedly I covered them with deer netting. Several are now blooming pink, red and orange. But I don't like the looks of netting and when I remove it, they will once again be vulnerable.

Trees that deer avoid in my garden are oak, pine, toyon, and *Podocarpus*.

Planting a garden attractive to ourselves and unattractive to deer requires thought and careful selection, but it can be done, gracefully.

~
CHAPTER SEVEN
~

*Low-Water Gardening*

# *Microclimates in the Garden*

~

Recently a very large, old Monterey pine was cut down just outside our garden. The shade it created had affected all the plants underneath its wide branches. As soon as that shade vanished, the character of that section of our garden changed. In garden lingo, from "dry shade" it became "dry sun." Over a period of weeks, I watched the branches of two salvia bushes, *Salvia clevelandii*, with their whorls of flowers and fragrant leaves, rotate. Previously, they had strained to the east to catch whatever rays of sun they could. Now they stretched to the south and west, evening out the general shape of the bushes, benefiting from their new exposure.

  This wordless response to increased sun made me think about microclimates in the garden—the importance of identifying them and the possibility for creation and change. One of the first classes in my Master Gardener course was about microclimates. The instructor used a light bulb on an extension cord—the sun—and the model of a house to impress upon us the difference in the amount of light the garden spaces on the east, west, north and south sides of the house receive throughout each day. Then she demonstrated how those differences are exaggerated as the seasons change and the angle of the sun decreases in winter, only to increase again in spring. The east side of the house is the first to feel the morning light. However, the south and west sides of the house receive light for more hours each day, and are thus warmer. The north side of the house receives the least light and is the coolest part of the garden.

Another aspect of microclimate is moisture. This is related to the amount of sun the garden receives, but is also affected by the type of soil and the slope of the garden. Clay soil retains moisture, whereas sandy soil does not. Ideally, our gardens would be filled with dark, crumbly loam which allows good drainage. My garden is not. I struggle with heavy clay, improving it slowly with compost, year by year.

Microclimate—and drainage—are also affected by slope. Just as water may pool in a low-lying spot in the garden, cold air will collect there. Cold air may also collect against a fence at the low end of the garden. Tender plants that might survive elsewhere may perish in a cold sink.

Wind is another aspect of microclimate. Plants in an open area, exposed to the wind, may suffer stress that plants in the lee of a fence or building, or sheltered by trees or shrubs, will not. But some plants, such as ornamental grasses, are healthy and at their most attractive swaying in the breeze.

We can take advantage of the microclimates created by our house, garage and fence. A south-facing brick wall, for example, will absorb heat during the day and release it slowly during the night. The may be the ideal place to plant a citrus tree, which will benefit from the longer period of warmth. When we lived in Colorado, my tomatoes thrived in a narrow garden strip along the south side of our brick garage. Here in Marin, I have planted roses in a south-facing raised bed. Behind it, a thick trumpet vine on a lattice offers further protection.

Choosing appropriate plants for each garden microclimate will also cut down on disease. Most plant diseases are non-pathenogenic. That means that they are not caused by pathogens such as viruses or infectious organisms, but by environmental factors. These noninfectious diseases can be quite serious; they may also weaken a plant so that it becomes susceptible to pathogens it might otherwise have resisted. For example, plants in wet patches may become diseased while their counterparts on a slope remain healthy. The environmental factors responsible for noninfectious diseases are temperature, moisture, light and condition of the soil—all important aspects of microclimates in the garden.

Understanding microclimates will influence which plants we put where. Choosing the right plant for the right space, we can enjoy a variety of plants in our gardens—and all can thrive.

# Drought-Tolerant Ferns

~

Drought-tolerant ferns—isn't that an oxymoron? When I think of ferns, I think of cool, damp spaces, shade, the sound of a creek gently burbling. That image is certainly true. Ferns do grow best in the shade. But it is also true that some species of ferns do not require a constant source of water. Hiking in California state parks, I have noted the profusion of a number of different species of ferns, growing lushly despite lack of artificial watering throughout the dry summer months.

In my own garden, I have planted sword ferns, the California native *Polystichum munitum*, among the most common drought-tolerant ferns. They thrive in the shade next to the east wall of our house. One large fern has grown and expanded and is begging to be divided. I am waiting until the fall rains start. That way, the newly-divided plants will benefit from our natural wet weather to reestablish their roots and will be prepared for next summer's dryness.

Although sword ferns commonly grow under redwoods in natural forests, they need little water once established. Sword ferns are also suitable for growing under oaks, which is to say, they are drought-tolerant. Sword ferns are widespread in the Bay area's open spaces, from deep forests to open hillsides. Regarding deer resistance, my own observation is that sword ferns are not the first choice of the deer that forage in my garden. However, the deer have neatly clipped the tender tips of some of the smaller ferns under our bay tree. The longer, tougher fronds are apparently not as palatable, and I think the sword ferns will survive without added protection.

There are a number of species of native California ferns sufficiently drought-tolerant to be suitable for growing under coast live oak (*Quercus agrifolia*) and Valley Oak (*Q. lobata*) trees. As our native oaks are susceptible to crown rot and oak root fungus, it is important that any plants under oaks not require much summer water.

In describing ferns, three terms are useful: fern leaves are called fronds, the leaflets of a frond are called pinnae, and the reproductive clusters along the margins of the leaf or lobes are called sori.

- California Maidenhair Fern (*Adiantum jordanii*) has stiff, wire-like stems lined with tiny, green-shaped leaflets or pinnae. It is native to southern Oregon and California. Growing as high as two feet tall, it has a delicate appearance consistent with its common name.

- Coffee Fern (*Pellaea andromedifolia*) is a small plant, growing to eighteen inches high. Unlike many ferns that have dark green foliage, the coffee fern's fronds range from gray-green to bluish-green. Its native habitat is southern Oregon and California. Although it doesn't need much water to survive, it may look dry during the summer months without occasional irrigation.

- Bird's Foot Fern (*Pellaea mucronata*) is related to—that is, in the same genus as—the Coffee Fern. It is larger than the Coffee Fern and derives its name from its distinctive foliage that consists of narrow leaflets arranged in groups of three. With some imagination, the fern's leaflets mirror the tracks of birds left in the sand.

- California Gold Back Fern (*Pentagramma triangularis*) has shiny brown or black stems with two- to five-inch fronds. Its pinnae are bright green above with a golden yellow underside, giving the fern its common name. The edges of he leaflets are slightly turned back which produce a three-dimensional effect. Dense, dark black sori contrast with the golden undersides.

- Bracken Fern (*Pteridium aquilinum*), a coarse, rough-looking fern, is native to many parts of the world. To me, it conjures up references to windswept moors in English novels. But it is also native to California. In Marin, I have seen it growing in thick patches as tall as four feet, although it may grow almost twice that high under some conditions. It is suitable for a garden with a natural, untamed look. It spreads by its deep rootstocks and is reputed to be potentially invasive. Some sources warn that the young fronds of bracken are not to be gathered to cook as fiddleheads; they contain a slow poison.

- Leather Leaf Fern (*Polypodium scouleri*) is the fern commonly used in flower arrangements. It is long-lasting and conveys the impression of natural woodlands in the vase indoors. Leather Leaf Fern is native from British Columbia to California. Its natural habitat is on trees and rocks, or growing in clumps in leaf mold in soil. It spreads by short rhizomes and will naturalize in the garden.

- California Wood Fern (*Dryopteris arguta*) is native all along the western coast from Washington to southern California. It may grow nearly three feet tall with wide spreading fronts that sway in the breeze. The pinnae remind me of many tiny oak leaves attached to a single long stem. It is a large, attractive fern, but may be difficult to grow in the garden.

- Licorice Fern (*Polypodium glycyrrhiza*), another California native, resembles a small version of the sword fern (*Polystichum munitum*) above. According to Donald Kirk's book, *Wild Edible Plants*, "the stem of the leaf, when chewed long enough, develops a distinct licorice flavor."

These ten species of ferns are all California natives with low water requirements. All are suitable for use in San Francisco Bay area gardens. By planting a selection of these shade-loving ferns, a feeling of lushness and native woodlands can grace any garden.

# Gardening without Watering

~

Once I attended a symposium of the Mediterranean Garden Society in Athens, Greece. It was entitled "The Dry Garden: Practice and Philosophy." One of the keynote speakers, Olivier Filippi, a nursery owner and garden philosopher from the south of France, made a deep impression on me. He and his wife have spent over twenty years collecting plants that grow wild in Mediterranean climates and propagating the plants for sale.

Filippi's basic premise is that if gardens in Mediterranean climates are planted with appropriately cultivated plants, they should not need any additional watering. What a relief that would be: no more overhead or drip irrigation systems to worry about! No bills for extra water for the garden! Not to mention the boon to the environment if precious water resources could be conserved for human use.

Most of us understand that lawns use a disproportionate amount of water and have reduced or eliminated them. Filippi goes one—or maybe several—steps farther.

He says, "The problem in gardens is not drought but rather the lack of knowledge on how to grow drought-resistant plants and on the proper gardening techniques suited to dry gardens."

In practice, what he advocates could be described as "tough love" for plants. His theory is that to establish a garden that does not require any additional water, the plants in the garden must have roots that grow deep enough to collect water from the ground during our dry summer months.

In order to develop those deep roots, plants must be conditioned from the time they are planted as seeds, or propagated as cuttings, to use their energy to develop roots rather than stems, leaves and flowers. This developmental dichotomy is referred to as "roots versus shoots." Traditionally, the root-to-shoot ratio in temperate climates is considered to be 1:1. That is, the size of the root system underneath the ground is equal to the size of the plant above the ground. By contrast, for example, a *Cistus* plant (Rock Rose), that grows one meter high in the wild may have a root system that is ten meters long.

Filippi's objective is to grow plants for cultivation that reflect this 10:1 ratio. Plants with roots this deep will be able to make use of water deep in the ground and not require additional summer water.

To develop long, straight roots in new plants, Filippi uses tall, narrow plastic containers with vertical ridges. A pot two inches across the top is ten inches deep. The vertical ridges prevent the spiraling roots so often found in nursery-grown plants. Once this spiral of roots is established—Filippi refers to it as a "chignon," like the hairstyle—it cannot straighten out. Even after a plant has been planted in a garden for years, its roots will be limited to growing in a tight spiral. As proof of this, Filippi produced a tall yucca plant that had fallen over: its roots were clustered in a tight ball. I recalled my own experience with a rhododendron that died in my garden. When I dug it up, its spiralled root ball looked the same as the day I had removed it from its nursery container and planted it several years before.

Once a young plant has developed straight ten-inch long roots in its container, it can be planted in the garden, preferably in the fall at the beginning of the rainy season. There, the root-to-shoot ratio is managed by trimming the plant back as close to the ground as possible for the first year – just as though it had been grazed by goats or deer. This is done so the new plant will spend as much of its energy as possible developing its roots. During its first summer, it should be watered slowly and deeply but infrequently: about seven gallons of water once every two weeks. In very dry circumstances, it could be given three and a half gallons of water once a week. After the first summer, the plant should require no water (in addition to natural rainfall) at all.

What the plant does require is trimming back twice a year. Trimming after flowering will keep the plant from using its energy to produce seeds. It also reduces the amount of leaves on the plant that lose moisture through evaporation during the hottest parts of summer.

To obtain plants that can develop deep roots, we need the help of local nurseries and commercial plant growers. Alternatively, gardeners can buy younger plants in smaller pots, before they have a chance to develop spiral roots and become root-bound in containers. Another is to propagate our own plants for our gardens, using tall, narrow pots. These pots are available from nurseries that focus on native plant restoration. It is no surprise to them that plants that are to survive in the wild need to develop long, straight roots.

Filippi has written a book entitled *Pour un jardin sans arrosage*, published in 2007 by Actes, Sud France. His book *Alternatives au gazon* has been translated into English as *Planting Design for Dry Gardens*. Online, Fillipi has published lovely photographs taken at his nursery near Beziers, France, and a number of plant lists using Latin names for plants appropriate for use in various sections of the unwatered garden.

# *Drought-Resistant Natives*

~

A friend gave me a booklet entitled "The Bee Pastures," a reprint of Chapter 16 of *The Mountains of California*, written by John Muir in 1894. Muir described California as "one sweet bee-garden throughout its entire length, north and south, and all the way across from the snowy Sierras to the ocean." He complained that "plows and sheep have made sad havoc in these glorious pastures" and deplored the large-scale cultivation of crops such as alfalfa and citrus that replaced the rich diversity of native plant life he had observed throughout the state. In the past one hundred twenty-five years, the situation has become much worse.

Honey bees and native pollinators, including butterflies and hummingbirds as well as solitary bees that do not produce honey, are responsible for pollinating most fruit and vegetable crops. Bees pollinate one hundred percent of California's valuable almond crop. But as most people are now aware, honey bees have recently been suffering from colony collapse disorder and native pollinators have been decimated by the indiscriminate use of pesticides and loss of habitat.

Muir noted that the chain of native blooming plants in California's "glorious pastures" continued throughout the year, and that is a goal to strive for in our own gardens:

- In February, Muir noted violets and numerous *Asteraceae*, which have flowers composed of clusters of flowers;

- In March, claytonia, calandrinia, white gilia and taller yellow composites bloom;
- In April, he observed the greatest height of bloom with a large variety of flowers;
- In May, it is lilies and California buckwheat;
- Muir refers to the summer months of June, July and August as "a winter of dry heat," when many native plants become dormant.
- In October, plants such as tarweed (*Hemizonia* species), asters and buckwheats bloom and provide sources of pollen and nectar that last through December.

Fall-blooming flowers are especially important to bees because the bees that are born in the fall are physiologically different from spring- and summer-born bees. Fall-born bees may live for as long as six months (as opposed to the seven-week life span of spring and summer bees), if they are well-nourished.

To provide the greatest benefits to pollinators, our gardens should include a variety of flowers in different sizes and shapes, so bees of different sizes and shapes can obtain pollen and nectar. Flowers should be grouped together, ideally in plots about four feet across. Blue, purple, white and yellow flowers seem to be the most attractive to bees. California native plants are characterized by requiring little maintenance and a minimum of water.

In my garden, natives including California poppies, mint, Santa Barbara daisies, ceanothus, salvias, zauschneria, verbena, monkeyflower, woodland strawberries and lilies, attract our own honey bees and many solitary bees as well. Mediterranean natives that thrive in our climate also provide excellent forage. A large patch of Spanish lavender hummed with bees in March. Now that those blossoms have faded, two large *Salvia clevelandii* bushes with their purple whorls of flowers are proving most attractive. Rosemary bushes and grevillea, which also thrive in our garden, are favorites of bees.

Other native plants attractive to native bees include asters, button bush, California redbud, columbine, lupine, phacelia, sunflower, manzanita, wild rose and willow. Non-natives include basil, cosmos, hyssop, marjoram and pincushion flowers.

As domestic gardeners, we can play a role in re-creating Muir's "sweet bee-garden" in our own small corners of Marin County by planting drought-resistant native species of flowers and shrubs that will provide pollen and nectar for pollinators.

## *Planting Under Oaks*

~

In the lower section of my sloping yard are three California live oak trees. One is old and venerable, the other two much younger. It is a section of our yard I have contemplated landscaping for several years. Last month railroad-tie steps were built to make the area accessible. An area was scraped and flattened for a garden bench. The loveliest feature of this garden section is the old oak tree. The challenge was to find plants that could fill the bare dirt around it without endangering its health. Coast live oaks flourish in our cool wet winters and warm dry summers. Over-watering is a serious health hazard. Oaks may develop crown root rot and oak root rot, soil-borne diseases fostered by moisture and warm temperatures. Understanding that, there are many native California plants and others that can thrive in the light shade and dry soil at the base of an oak.

For ground cover on our garden slope, I chose the low-growing *Ceanothus, C. hearstiorum,* which spreads in a star-like configuration and has tiny dark green leaves. Its spring flowers are medium blue—the small shapely cones of the wild lilac. This *Ceanothus* was discovered on the grounds of Hearst Castle in southern California. I was told it is considered a rare and endangered species. The chance to plant and possess my own reputed rare and endangered California native intrigues me. I planted five. In two or three years, they will cover their allotted space. *Ceanothus* are also susceptible to root rot if over-watered. They often grow naturally on rocky slopes and go without water all summer long. This makes them perfect partners for oaks. I will carefully water mine this first summer, only until they are established.

I planted another California native, island alum root, not far away. This heuchera (*Heuchera maxima*) is reputed to grow up to two feet across—one nursery told me three! Its flowers consist of hundreds of tiny coral bells hovering on thin stems above its large roundish leaves. This native of the Channel Islands is new to my garden and I am already imagining its eventual glorious size.

Douglas iris (*Iris douglasiana*) and the Pacific Coast Hybrid iris (*I.* 'PCH') in their lovely pale colors will provide more spring color. Their long, pointed leaves contrast with the texture of the large heuchera leaves and the tiny dark green leaves of the ceanothus.

For a more delicate ground cover under the oaks, I could have chosen wood strawberries (*Fragaria californica*). These tough natives spread by runners that grow in all directions, eventually forming a mat difficult for weeds to invade. Birds find their seedy fruit delicious.

Monkey flower bushes (*Mimulus aurantiacus*) flower during the spring and summer. Their funnel-shaped blossoms have two lips said to resemble a monkey's grinning face. Three I bought at the California Native Plant Society's plant sale in the fall were just beginning to bloom in May. The first to bloom this spring is cream-colored. The bushes with orange and bronze flowers will bloom later on.

To add summer color under the oaks, I planted three non-native species. These gave me particular pleasure because I was able to obtain them by dividing mature plants from other parts of my garden. Along the fence, I planted a row of bronze daylilies (*Hemerocallus*). They are very hardy with a long blooming season. Among the ceanothus, I planted several dwarf yellow daylilies whose height is in keeping with the low-growing ground cover. Along the path, still shaded by the oaks, I planted summer-blooming red-hot pokers (*Kniphofia uvaria*). Hummingbirds are attracted to the bright tubular flowers. The graceful arching leaves of all these plants are a pleasure even when they are not in bloom. Along a two-railroad-tie-high wall, I planted four rosemary bushes of the prostratus type (*Rosmarinus* 'Huntington Blue'). Although they grow only eighteen inches high, they will trail over the wall, becoming a gray-green curtain with tiny pale blue flowers. The flowers attract both birds and bees, and I often clip fresh sprigs of rosemary to use as a bed under salmon I am grilling. Rosemary is a Mediterranean native that endures hot sun, poor soil, and requires no irrigation.

Other non-natives in my garden that would also do well under oaks include catmint (*Nepeta faassenii*) with its gray-green foliage and delicate purple flower spikes; Santa Barbara daisy (*Erigeron karvinskianus*) with its summer-long white flowers on dark mounds of foliage; lavender cotton (*Santolina chamaecyparissus*), a silver gray hill of foliage with bright yellow flowers in late spring; grevillea (*Grevillea rosmarinifolia*) with its needle-like green foliage and intricate rose and cream winter blossoms; various yarrows (*Achillea*) with gray or green foliage, depending on the variety, and tight flower umbels of white, yellow, salmon or brick (some *Achillea* are native Californians, others not).

To respect the oak, plants should not be placed too close to the trunk—six to ten feet is close enough. To grow plants successfully under oaks, minimize disturbance of the oaks' root zone, minimize soil movement, and carefully target the root systems of the new plants when watering. With some thought and care, under oaks a lovely garden can bloom.

# Thriving in Clay Soil

~

California life oaks (*Quercus agrifolia*) and valley oaks (*Q. lobata*) live happily in clay soil. But what is good for oaks presents a challenge to many plants: it is difficult for plants to extend their roots through the tiny, densely-packed particles. Water molecules get stuck, retained for much longer in clay than they are in sandy soil. Air has a tough time penetrating, too. What can a gardener do?

One solution is to change the character of the soil in the garden by amending it with either organic or inorganic materials. Another solution is to choose plants for the garden that are naturally adapted to clay soils.

My hillside garden is dominated by a live oak tree. The soil throughout my garden is clay. I have chosen plants that are adapted to the existing soil. However, I am also mulching liberally with shredded bark each year. I find that, year by year, as the mulch breaks down, it adds a new layer to the soil. By mulching, I am gradually changing the character of the clay soil. In the meantime, several species of native California plants have proven especially successful in my garden.

*Salvia clevelandii* is one of my favorites. I first encountered it on a hike near Muir Beach. In the warm afternoon sun, the unmistakable fragrance of the leaves perfumed the air. The bushes were thriving along the roadside. Their whorled lavender-colored blossoms encircled the long stems like delicate rings. What a plus to discover that the bushes I bought at the nursery thrive in clay soil!

~ *Low-Water Gardening* ~

Another native that I met on the open slopes of Mt. Tam, sticky monkey flower (*Mimulus aurantiacus*), also grows well in clay soil. Bright orange flowers peek out of the dark green foliage of these bushes in the spring. I have planted several of these in my lower garden where they please me year after year. The common monkey flower (*M. guttatus*) likes clay soil, too.

The feathery silver foliage of Sandhill sage (*Artemesia pyncocephala*) brightens the edge of the path down my hill. *Artemesia* prefer full sun. Their rounded forms contrast with the stiff upright fans of African iris, also called fortnight lilies (*Dietes*), growing nearby. Although fortnight lilies are reputed to require fairly good soil, they have naturalized bountifully in my clay soil.

California wild lilacs (*Ceanothus*) tolerate clay soil and generally harsh conditions. In the wild, they grow on rocky slopes and go without surface water all summer. In the garden, their biggest enemy is too much water, which can cause root rot. I have planted two varieties of *Ceanothus* in the clay soil under my oaks: Carmel Creeper (*C. griseus horizontalis*) and one other, discovered on the grounds of the Hearst Castle, *C. hearstiorum*. Both have purple blossoms in the spring. I find the shiny, round green foliage of Carmel Creeper particularly appealing.

In addition to these shrubs, I have a number of native herbaceous perennials that do well in clay soil. These include the plants I think of as the *Sisyrinchium* sisters, blue-eyed grass (*S. bellum*) and yellow-eyed grass (*S. californicum*). Unfortunately, when I planted them, I didn't realize that although blue-eyed grass does well in dry areas, yellow-eyed grass prefers wetter places. Half my yellow-eyed grass perished for lack of water.

In a sunny section of my garden, common thrift (*Armeria maritima*) grows well enough in the clay soil; however, I have read that *Armeria* require excellent soil drainage. If that is the case, the very nature of clay soil, to trap water and hold it, may explain why my thrift is not truly thriving.

Various yarrows (*Achilleas*) are very tolerant of clay soil. These sun-loving plants are some of my favorites for their wide range of flower color and many medicinal properties.

Finally, another Southwest native that is doing very well in my clay soil is *Gaura* (*G. lindheimeri*). I have heard this plant called "butterflies-in-the-wind" and that is just what it looks like. One-inch-long white and pink blossoms open on long, nearly invisible stems above a mound of long green leaves. The blossoms appear to be floating and dancing in the breeze. The plants prefer full sun and continue blooming all summer. *Gaura* is reputed to self-seed. I anxiously anticipate this development.

When planting, especially in clay soil, it is important to avoid injury to the roots of plants. Soil should not be compacted too tightly around them. Water should not collect around the base of the plant. If planting near oak trees, respect the needs of the oak. Don't plant within six feet of the trunk of the oak, and then plant only species that don't require much irrigation.

There are many native California plants adapted to clay soils. This small sampling shows that by choosing the right plants, we can garden successfully in clay.

~

CHAPTER EIGHT

~

*Back To Basics*

# *Weed Identification and Control*

~

The plentiful rains this spring have produced an especially vibrant crop of weeds in my garden. In between showers, I have been pulling them out. As I work, I contemplate what I know about the various species. Knowing the enemy in this case is essential to controlling it.

Weeds can be defined as any misplaced plants. For example, a tomato plant is welcome in the kitchen vegetable garden, but is a weed in the front flower border. However, weeds are also defined by their characteristic competitiveness, persistence and perniciousness. Weeds produce abundant seeds that may survive in a dormant state for long periods of time. They establish populations rapidly, easily occupy disturbed sites and have developed multiple methods for spreading vegetatively. They are tough enough to out-compete the plants we are trying to cultivate in our gardens. Thus, we engage in the ongoing struggle to bring them under control.

**Weed Identification**

Identifying weeds is key to controlling them. It is important to understand their life cycles, how they grow and develop. Just as other plants in our gardens, weeds can be divided into annuals, biennials and perennials. Annuals grow, set seed and die in one year or less. They may be either winter annuals that germinate in the fall, live through the winter and produce seed in the winter and spring, or summer annuals that germinate in the spring and produce seed in summer or fall. Winter annuals include mallow, groundsel and annual bluegrass. Summer annuals include lamb's quarters, spotted spurge, crabgrass and pigweed.

Biennials take two years to complete their life cycles. In the first year, they produce leaves, stems and roots. In the spring and summer of the second year, they flower, set seed and die. They are easier to control than annuals because we usually discover and eliminate them from our gardens during their first year of growth, before they have a chance to set seed and spread. Examples of biennial weeds include mullein, bull thistle, ox tongue and shepherd's purse.

Perennial weeds live longer than two years and develop more extensive root systems than annuals or biennials. Young perennials may be pulled or hoed out. However, once they are established, they are difficult to eradicate. Simple perennials, such as dandelions, reproduce only by seed. Creeping perennials, such as wood sorrel (*Oxalis*) and Bermuda grass, spread aggressively via underground structures including stolons, rhizomes, tubers and bulbs. They may be dormant over winter and send out new shoots in the spring. Other perennial weeds are nutsedge, broom, bindweed and poison oak.

From the point of view of plant taxonomy, weeds can be divided into broadleafs (dicots) or grasses (monocots). Thus, there are annual, biennial and perennial broadleafs and annual, biennial and perennial grasses.

As I work to eliminate the weeds in my garden, I try to pull out annuals before they have a chance to go to seed. Biennials must go at first appearance. I dig out perennials like dandelions and *Oxalis* and poison oak, capturing as much of the root systems as possible. Knowing something about weeds' life cycles increases my understanding of their characteristics. It doesn't make the work easier, but by putting names to the weeds and learning something about them, I develop a relationship with them. As I learn more about all the plants in my garden, I find more pleasure in the endless endeavor of creating and maintaining it.

## Weed Control

As interesting as it is to know the names of various weeds and whether they are annuals, biennials or perennials, my real motivation in getting to know them is to determine how to control them. I would like to eliminate weeds completely from my garden, but given the competitive advantages weeds enjoy, producing thousands of seeds or hundreds of underground tubers each year (one yellow nutsedge plant can make four hundred new tubers in one year), I will settle for some level of weeds I can control using the various means available.

There are four basic categories of weed control: cultural, mechanical, physical and chemical.

### Cultural

The point of cultural weed control is to modify the garden environment to increase the desirable plants' competitive edge while decreasing the competitive advantage of weeds. The selection of plants is critical. By choosing among the many plants that naturally thrive in our garden's climate, we immediately improve the garden's edge over weeds.

The condition of the garden's soil is another cultural factor. Know whether your garden soil is clay or sand or loam and choose plants that prefer your existing soil type, or modify the soil by adding organic matter such as compost to make it a better home for the plants you prefer.

Prepare the soil for planting by loosening it, so oxygen will be available for plants' roots to grow. Similarly, reduce soil compaction by watching where you step in the garden. Trampling the garden squeezes the spaces out of the soil, spaces necessary for the flow of air and water, and growth of roots.

Proper irrigation is another cultural factor in weed control. Over-watering may encourage the germination of weed seeds, whereas under-watering may stress plants and allow weeds to move in.

Lawns should be watered deeply and infrequently to discourage weeds such as crabgrass. Thatch should be removed if it gets over one-half inch thick. Mowing height is also important. A key rule is to never remove more than one-third of the leaf blade in a simple mowing. "Scalping" a lawn allows weeds to germinate and grow.

### Mechanical

These are the tried-and-true, time-honored techniques of weed control: hoeing, cultivating, hand-pulling, mowing and chopping. They are non-polluting and require no elaborate equipment. In my garden, combined with the cultural and physical weed control methods, I also spend some time each week hand-pulling and digging, which keeps weeds down to a tolerable level.

For annual weeds, the main objective is to get them out before they set seed. Using a dandelion digger, I cut them below their crowns, just beneath the soil level. Perennial weeds required repeated digging out. The theory is that eventually their roots will be starved for food and will die out. Persistence is the key. It may require several years of digging up perennial weeds to starve them out.

An old rhyme, "Water, wait, then cultivate," describes a mechanical system for controlling weeds. Before planting a bed, prepare it to finished grade, then water it to germinate the weed seeds that are already present. Wait until the weeds sprout, then, using a hoe, get rid of them. For best results, repeat the process a second time. When you do plant your garden seeds, disturb the soil as little as possible to avoid bringing more weed seeds to the surface.

**Physical**

Physical weed control means placing a barrier between weed seeds and the sun. Without light, there is no photosynthesis and weeds can't grow. A physical barrier is usually mulch. Mulch may be organic, such as ground bark, straw or compost, or inorganic, such as commercial weed blocks or black polyethylene plastic.

Mulch is a very effective way to control weeds. I have been using shredded bark in my garden for several years. Over time it breaks down, adding organic matter to the soil, and I add a new layer. I can tell how effective it is because in the farthest corner of my garden, where the mulch is very thin, a significant number of weeds flourish. I have pulled them out again this year, but putting down a thick, three- to six-inch layer of mulch would save me a lot of time next spring.

Mulch also saves water. With a covering of mulch, soil stays moist longer, so adjust watering accordingly. Overwatering may result in root rot development from *Phytophthora* or *Pythium fungi*.

## Chemical

Chemical weed control, that is, use of herbicides, should be the last resort. Herbicides are organic and inorganic chemicals that kill plants. They may be sprayed on weed foliage or applied to the soil. They may be pre-emergent, or soil-residual herbicides, that prevent the germination of weed seeds, or post-emergent, applied to weed foliage. Post-emergent herbicides may be contact herbicides that kill only the parts of plants they touch, or systemic herbicides that are absorbed into the plant and move through the plant's conductive tissues to affect another site, such as the plant's roots.

Herbicides may be nonselective, killing all vegetation, or selective, killing only susceptible species (presumably the weeds) and not damaging the tolerant species (the garden plants). Unfortunately, selectivity is relative, not absolute, and environmental conditions may make tolerant species susceptible to even selective herbicides. And herbicides we use in our gardens may end up polluting our water.

We may never completely eliminate weeds in our gardens, but by understanding something about weeds and the various means available to control them—cultural, mechanical, physical and chemical—we may transform them into less formidable foes.

# *Poisonous Garden Plants*

~

Recently, I helped a friend weed her garden. It is largely native California plants and abuts public land. I wore gloves and was on the lookout for poison oak. I didn't see any at all. However, the next day my forearms were covered with an itchy red rash. Consulting the *California Master Gardener Handbook*, I learned that my dermatitis—that is, an inflammation of the skin accompanied by redness, itching, and tenderness to touch—could have been caused by a number of plants I had never considered.

Dermatitis caused by plants is divided into two categories: allergic contact dermatitis and irritant contact dermatitis.

Allergic contact dermatitis only affects folks who are sensitized to the plant material or allergen. Allergic individuals are sensitized by their first encounter with the plant. Their bodies respond by producing white blood cells that recognize the allergen. Subsequent encounters with the allergen result in redness, itching, and blisters. Fortunately, injury is limited to the skin area exposed to the plant material. Many people are allergic to members of the *Rhus* genus, which includes poison oak, poison ivy and poison sumac. However, there are numerous other plants that can cause allergic contact dermatitis. These include asters, birch, tulip and narcissus bulbs, carrots, cedar trees, celery, chrysanthemums, English ivy, garlic, ginger, magnolias, oleanders, onions, pine trees and primrose.

Irritant contact dermatitis is nonallergic, inflammatory skin reactions or rash caused by chemicals contained in plant material. Although not everyone will suffer the allergic reactions described above, everyone is susceptible to irritant dermatitis caused by certain plants. For example, plants such as philodendron, pothos and diffenbachia, members of the Arum family, have special cells that contain oxalic acid crystals. When a leaf is brushed or broken, these cells contract and eject the oxalic acid crystals with enough force to embed them in a person's skin, causing serious irritation. If the crystals penetrate a person's mucous membranes, they can cause intense burning and irritation very destructive to the kidneys. Other plants that cause irritant contact dermatitis include century plant, cowslip, cucumber, species of *Ficus*, foxglove, milkweed, parsley, parsnip, poinsettia, tomato and turnip.

An interesting variation on allergic contact dermatitis is photosensitization dermatitis. This type of dermatitis is caused by plants containing chemicals that injure the skin only when activated by sunlight. It can occur either in livestock, injured when they graze on plants that contain these chemicals, or in humans allergic to them. Derivatives of toxins produced by these plants are called furocoumarins that permanently darken the skin after contact. Medicine has found a use for furocoumarins in treating people with abnormally light pigmentation. Plants that may cause photosensitization dermatitis in humans include buttercup, carrots, celery with pink rot, dill, figs, Klamath weed, lime and other citrus rinds, mustard and parsley.

The initial treatment for plant-caused dermatitis is to wash the exposed skin thoroughly with soap and cold water. There are some specialized commercial soaps which claim to be particularly effective against allergens like poison oak. Physically removing the plant chemicals causing the irritation by washing is the most effective way to limit damage to the skin.

Once the damage has been sustained, one can only treat the symptoms. Topical anesthetics containing benzocaine may relieve itching, but it is also possible to develop an allergic reaction to the medication—in addition to the original reaction. Topical antihistamines, topical antibiotics, and topical mercury compounds such as mercurochrome may also provide some relief, although sensitive individuals may experience allergic reactions to them as well.

The best way to deal with plant-caused dermatitis is to prevent it, rather than try to treat it. Protect your skin in the garden by wearing gloves, long-sleeved shirts, long pants, and socks. One shouldn't have to pay a penalty for the pleasure of spending time working with plants in the garden.

# Soil Drainage: Spaces In-between
~

The clay soil in my garden is pretty much solid. Or so I thought, until I began reflecting on soil and what it really is—the particles that compose soil and the importance of the spaces in-between. Soil experts have names for these: the particles of soil are referred to as the solid phase; the spaces in between are called the pore space.

The mineral particles that make up soil can be categorized by size. The tiniest particles are called clay. Medium-size particles are called silt. Large particles are called sand. When clay soil is moist, you can form it into a ball and then squeeze it into a ribbon between your fingers and it will retain its shape. By contrast, if you try to form a ribbon of sand in your hand, it will fall apart. Silt is somewhere in between.

The size of the soil particles determines how much pore space there is for air and water. Tiny clay particles get so packed together that water cannot flow through them. Sand particles have so much space between them that water flows through practically unimpeded. The roots of plants planted in clay soil may suffer from over-watering and rot because water remains caught in the soil, whereas plants planted in sandy soil may dry out because they cannot capture sufficient water as it passes through the soil.

The ideal soil for many plants is loam. That is the dark, crumbly soil that contains not only mineral particles but also particles of organic matter, such as decaying leaves. By mixing compost—decaying leaves and other organic matter—into soil, whether clay or silt or sand, we can moderate the rate at which soil drains. Adding compost to clay soil will cause it to drain more quickly, whereas adding compost to sandy soil will help the sandy soil retain moisture and drain more slowly.

The space in-between the mineral particles of soil—the pore space—also controls the level of air flow to plants' roots. Plants require air to grow. Unlike animals, plants use the carbon dioxide in the air to create carbohydrates and create oxygen as their respiratory waste product.

Ideally, soil also provides nourishment for organisms such as earthworms that reside there. Organic matter, such as compost, provides nutrients for the animals and bacteria and fungus that live in the soil.

According to the *California Master Gardener Handbook*, the four principal components of soil with ideal moisture content for plant growth are: a pore space consisting of twenty-five percent water and twenty-five percent air; and a solid phase consisting of forty-five percent minerals and five percent organic matter.

Even after we conscientiously mix organic matter into the soil in our gardens, we will still have either a basically clay or sandy soil. To develop a thriving garden, we must choose plants compatible with the type of soil we have.

When gardening in containers, it is easier to control the quality of the soil. Commercially available potting soils contain bark or wood chips to hold water and create air pockets, and sand or vermiculite to provide structure. Potting soil will become worn out over time, that is, the minerals will have been used by the plant or have been washed out by continued watering. A soluble fertilizer will help replace missing minerals. Plants should be repotted with new soil when they outgrow their containers. When potting or repotting, if soil falls out of the drainage hole in the bottom of the container, a few broken pot shards can be placed over drainage holes to prevent soil loss. Any container in which plants are grown must have drainage holes. Soil should be as close as possible to the ideal mixture given above in order to drain properly.

Whether we are gardening in a plot of ground or in containers on the balcony, the quality of the soil provides the basis for the health of our plants. Think about the type of particles that make up the soil, and remember the importance of the spaces in-between.

# *Rerouting Rain Runoff*

~

Before man began constructing buildings and paving roads and parking lots, when rain fell on the earth it percolated down through layers of sand and soil and eventually entered the water table below the surface. When rain falls on solid buildings and paved surfaces, it runs around them often causing serious erosion. In modern cities, this runoff water is collected in storm drains which route the runoff to the nearest body of water.

In the San Francisco Bay Area, storm drains typically flow into streams and eventually flow into the bay. Storm drains, which are expensive to build, collect water often containing petrochemicals, pesticides and herbicides. The runoff is often warmer in temperature than the water in the rivers, streams, lakes or ocean into which the runoff flows. Adding polluted or warmer water to natural water bodies causes changes in their ecology, sometimes killing native species or causing destructive plant or algae growth.

In 1990, while designing a subdivision in Prince George's County in Maryland, David Brinker developed a plan to collect rainwater in gardens, rather than allowing it to run off into storm drains or be collected in a storage pond. One immediate benefit of these "rain gardens" was economic: the cost to build storm drains for the subdivision would have been $400,000. The complete cost of the rain gardens was $100,000.

The gardens were aesthetically pleasing, and the water was retained in the local soil. The rain gardens reduced storm water runoff from seventy-five to eighty percent, according to flow monitoring done in later years. These prototype rain gardens spawned a whole landscaping movement now known as Low Impact Development.

The concept of rain gardens is simple:

- Identify where water will run off a building or parking lot.

- Plant gardens that will contain the water long enough for it to sink into the ground. Homeowners may check the drain spouts from the gutters that run along the edge of their roof. A pipe may be used to carry the water away from the foundation of the house to a garden area.

Make sure the plants in this area can tolerate damp roots during the rainy season of the year. Robust native plants that grow at the edge of wetlands, such as sedges, rushes, ferns, select shrubs and small trees, will do well in these conditions. If a low-lying area will contain water much of the time, it is called a wetlands rather than a rain garden. Rain gardens allow water to infiltrate—sink into—the ground in about forty-eight hours.

Commercial buildings and parking lots are more complex, but the principle is the same. Raised berms or depressed swales may be used to contain and collect water. In order to obtain a commercial building permit, the applicant must demonstrate how runoff will be dealt with.

In one case I am familiar with, the original plan called for the use of permeable paving stones in the parking lot rather than impermeable asphalt. A thoughtful alternative landscaping plan using a series of planted berms to keep the water inside the property and out of the storm drains provided a much more economical solution.

One doesn't have to be a subdivision developer or a commercial contractor, however, to take a step toward keeping rainfall from running into storm drains. The first step is conscious awareness: each householder should examine his or her own property to determine where runoff goes. The second step is to find a way to create a rain garden to capture the runoff and, using the appropriate plants, retain the water in the soil.

# Sowing Seeds

~

When the California poppies in my garden completed their splashy spring show, I gathered their crescent-moon-shaped seed pods in a paper bag. The ripe pods burst as they fell into the bag, though some exploded prematurely on the ground. Happily, I ended up with a substantial seed harvest.

Now it is time to plant them. Theodore Payne, who ran a nursery and seed business from 1903 to 1958 promoting California native plants, noted that "a mixture of wildflower seeds, providing it contains a sufficient number of species, and the correct proportion of each, is preferable to one kind of flower, for the reason that it will produce a succession of flowers over a longer period."

I share his vision of a seasonal succession of native blooms for my own garden. In addition to my hand-gathered California poppies, I will be planting *Clarkia*, baby blue-eyes, *Gilia*, lupine, tidy-tips and more.

Now is the time to take advantage of the fall rains, which will allow wildflower seeds to germinate without extra watering. Many native plants are drought-tolerant, but they require sufficient water to germinate, develop and become established before our next dry summer sets in.

In her book *Gardening with a Wild Heart*, Judith Larner Lowry emphasizes the importance of creating a weed-free seedbed, by either rototilling or hand- digging before planting. This will give the young seedlings at least a fair chance of success as they compete to survive.

To produce the feeling of a meadow of wildflowers or a natural-looking border, mix native plant seed with at least four times the amount of fine sand or potting soil, then broadcast it over the area in sweeping arm gestures.

To discourage birds from eating the seed, walk over the area. The pressure of your feet will settle the seed sufficiently deep. To tamp down large areas, you may put down a sheet of cardboard and walk on it. In Glenn Keator's book *The Complete Garden Guide to the Native Perennials of California*, he breaks down the handling of seeds into five components: seed storage, cleaning, pretreatment, planting and seedling establishment.

For seed storage, Keator suggests glass jars, and points out that seeds stored for the shortest time are most viable.

Note that seed pods and other chaff can contain fungal spores that may kill young seedlings, so clean the seed you gather yourself.

Some seeds also require pretreatment (described below) in order to break their dormancy.

Planting may be done directly into the garden as described above, or seeds may be planted in shallow flats or pots. Commercial potting mixes are pest-free and provide good aeration. Planting depth should be one to two times the diameter of the seed. Water frequently so soil remains damp but not soggy.

Seedling establishment refers to transplanting young plants from a flat either to an intermediate pot or directly to the garden once it has several sets of true leaves.

In Marjorie Schmidt's classic *Growing California Native Plants*, she says that, although "a large proportion germinate readily without pretreatment of seed, including practically all annuals, many perennials and biennials," some pretreatment is required for seeds that resist germination.

*~ Back To Basics ~*

Pretreatments include scarification, hot-water treatment, burning and cold stratification.

- Scarification is used to break the seed coat of some members of the legume family. Small amounts of seed may be rubbed between two pieces of sandpaper, and larger seeds may be perforated with a file or knife.

- Hot water (180 degrees Fahrenheit) is used to cover seeds such as redbud and lupine, then allowed to cool overnight. Once soaked, seeds must be planted immediately.

- Burning can be accomplished by spreading pine needles over a flat planted with seeds such as matilija poppy, manzanita and red thistle. Set the pine needles on fire and allow them to burn down. Water well after the flat has cooled.

- Cold stratification is used to overcome internal dormancy in some seeds. Seeds such as incense cedar or desert mahogany are mixed with moist sand, peat moss or sphagnum moss and placed in plastic bags. When the seed swells, it is ready to plant. Note that bags may be placed in the refrigerator for one to two months.

For me, one of the pleasures of gardening is reading about other gardeners' experiences. Other books on growing native plants from seed include *Seed Propagation of Native California Plants* by Dara E. Emery and *Gardener's Guide to California Wildflowers* by Kevin Connelly.

# *A Place for Invasives?*

~

Is there ever a time to plant invasives—plants that are known to spread—in the garden? I believe the answer is a qualified "yes."

There is never a time to plant exotic, that is non-native, invasives. Exotic invasives such as pampas grass and French and Scottish broom were sold by local nurseries in the past, before their destructive nature was understood. Plants like these are so hardy they replace California natives in open spaces. Today, for example, volunteers spend hundreds of hours pulling out broom growing on Mt. Tamalpais in an effort to recreate an environment conducive to California native plants. There is no place for exotic invasives in California and they should be pulled out or dug up and destroyed.

Native invasive plants are another story: there are situations in which they can be both practical and desirable. In my garden, I have a lot of space to fill. As I select plants for inclusion, I look for California natives and Mediterranean species that will reproduce or expand naturally in our San Francisco Bay area climate. It is the rate at which some plants reproduce that qualifies them as invasives: they will invade the empty spaces of my garden over time. Some send out roots that can sprout leaves, other reproduce by rhizomes, some produce easily germinating seeds, some send out runners. Planting invasives is a calculated risk. I have learned that the invasion of my garden is a slow march at best.

*~ Back To Basics ~*

## California Natives

**Woodland strawberry:** This year I had all the ivy removed from my garden. Like mint, each node on each shoot of ivy is capable of growing its own roots and sprouting leaves if it is in contact with the soil. So even though the ivy has been removed once, I will have to be vigilant in pulling up any new shoots I see. I searched for a native plant that could successfully compete against ivy. The apparently delicate *Fragaria californica*, or woodland strawberry, is reputed to be tough enough. Once it establishes itself as a mat of interlocking runners of adjacent plants, it should keep the ivy out. So far, the half dozen I planted have produced tiny new plants that are rooting and extending additional runners out about three feet in diameter around each plant.

**Redwood sorrel:** The trait which makes the exotic *Oxalis pexcaprae* (formerly *O. cernua*), Bermuda buttercup, a troublesome weed, makes its native cousin *Oxalis oregana*, redwood sorrel, desirable in my garden. When we ripped out the ivy underneath our redwood tree, again I searched for something tough. Redwood sorrel, as the name suggests, is a native of coastal forests from Washington to California, and a logical choice for this spot. It is a larger plant, with broader leaves and showier white or pink flowers than its weedy relative. The time I spend pulling *Oxalis cernua* out of my garden made me pause when I considered planting *Oxalis oregana* under the redwood. Although redwood sorrel is not as prolific in putting out roots that will sprout into new plants as its relative, I am very pleased with my choice.

**California fuchsia:** Another invasive which I have planted is the California native *Epilobium canum* (formerly *Zauschneria californica*), also known as California fuchsia. Its dusty gray foliage has a wild and rangy look about it.

However, the brilliant scarlet trumpet-shaped flowers are a great favorite of hummingbirds. I planted these fuchsias for the birds' enjoyment. Two seasons after I planted them, I noticed numerous gray wisps of plants emerging in the general vicinity of the older plants. A few of these I allowed to stay and maybe they will succeed. But others I pulled up as weeds. That certainly is one way to deal with any invasives. Or, if you find you suffer an embarrassment of riches in terms of free new plants, you can always dig them up and give them away.

### Mediterranean Species

**Valerian:** I planted valerian, *Centhranthus ruber*, because I admire its plentiful pink spikes of blossoms in springtime. I have seen it proliferating in road cuts and on steep dry banks. I like it because it is an herb with medicinal properties, primarily known for its calming, sleep-inducing effects. Despite its reputation as an invasive, only a few new young plants have sprouted around the bases of the four I originally planted. I look forward to a large block of plants developing.

**Erigeron:** Although it is commonly called Santa Barbara daisy, *Erigeron karvinskianus* is a native of Mexico. Considered an invasive plant, I have found it more prolific in self-seeding than the valerian. Often it appears that a single plant is increasing its diameter, but when I lift up the edges of the plant I discover that new plants have sprouted under the cover of the mother plant, producing, in effect, a colony. To my delight, the mounds of small pink and white blossoms are expanding.

**Mint:** Spearmint, *Mentha spicata*, in my garden, as well as many other species of mint, is aggressively invasive. I find myself pulling mint out of the area in which it serves as a ground cover, treating it as a weed when it moves to spots where I am encouraging other plants. On other occasions, I clip it to flavor tea or use in a salad or savory dish. In every case, I appreciate its fragrance and its glossy green foliage and I'm happy to have it in abundant supply.

# *Dividing and Multiplying*

~

In order to install some plants in a raised bed, I had to dig up six large daylilies. It had been several years since I had divided them and they were large enough to divide again. Splitting each clump in half gave me twelve: seven for one side of a garden path and five for the other. As I planted the daylilies, I started looking at the existing plants in my garden with new eyes. I saw a wealth of plant material waiting to be redistributed.

My goal is to transform my garden from spare to lush —spending a minimum of money, concentrating on plants that need minimal water. I already have an assortment of low-water plants: salvias, lavenders, rosemaries, fortnight lilies, sword ferns, daylilies, red hot pokers (*Kniphofia*), *Crocosmia*, Gladwin iris and *Achilleas*.

During a recent deer attack, those voracious eaters destroyed three *Ceanothus* I had been fostering as ground cover under an aging oak. Daylilies (*Hemerocallis*), requiring a minimum of water, are acceptable for planting under oaks, so I decided to use some plant divisions there. My daylilies fall into two categories: the old-fashioned bronze-colored flowers I replanted along the path, and newer, named varieties. Under the oak, I planted 'Kelly's Girl' and 'Nile Crane,' as well as 'Cranberry Baby' and a dwarf yellow. My neighbor had asked for some 'Kelly's Girl,' which I was able to share with her.

To divide the clumps of daylilies, I used a shovel and a garden fork. I located a likely-looking line for the division and slid the fork between the individual plants. Wiggling the fork back and forth loosened the dirt and the bonds between the daylilies' tuberous roots. To pull the sections apart, I resorted to brute force. The indignity of division seems harsh, but I know that the new plants will appreciate the room and opportunity to grow.

Near the newly-replanted daylilies thrives a large patch of Mexican bush sage (*Salvia leucantha*). Over the years, I have distributed clumps of Mexican sage around the garden. It is time to dig up sections of new shoots growing around the mother plant and move them to places they will receive sufficient light. It seems to take Mexican sage a season or two to recover from the shock of being moved, but these plants are tough.

In the tough category, fortnight lilies (*Dietes*), also known as African iris, are especially easy to divide and grow. They have nearly become invasive in my unfenced upper garden. Deer do not eat their sword-like leaves. The plants provide an upright structural line in the garden, contrasting nicely with the arched leaves of daylilies and branches of rosemary. I just dig up a clump of fortnight lilies and, once again using a garden fork and shovel, pry the fans apart. In an empty space between a flight of steps and the anti-deer fence in the lower garden, I planted a row of fortnight lilies, interspersed with Santa Barbara daisies (*Erigeron*). The daisies were sprouting up as wayward volunteers in places they do not belong. I dug them up and replanted them. They will be both useful and attractive in their new home.

Similarly, I have Spanish lavender plants that have sprouted from seed. Some of the small plants are in the right place to supersede older plants now declining. But others, particularly those growing up in the middle of the gravel path, must migrate. I dig them up carefully, hoping to preserve as many of their tiny roots as possible and gently plant them where they may thrive.

Rosemary plants, of several varieties, are spreading spectacularly and sending out branches that root as they touch the ground. Some of these are covering empty spaces admirably; others crowd their neighbors. The newly-rooted plant can be moved by cutting the umbilical-like branch that links it to the mother plant and digging up a generous amount of earth around its roots.

Another favorite is my 'Coronation Gold' *Achillea*. It produces offspring along its stems. Using metal staples to pin the stems with the baby plants to the ground, they have taken root.

In addition to these plants, I have clumps of *Kniphofia* ready to divide, just like daylilies. Sword ferns can be divided in clumps, or new plants can be separated from runners. And a few years ago, my sister-in-law brought me a bundle of *Crocosima* and Gladwin iris from her garden. I planted them all. Now the iris are ready to divide. The *Crocosima* have spread by corms that I can dig up and replant in other areas.

The abundance of dividable plants I have identified gives me an opportunity to move plants around my own garden and also repay my friends' generosity by sharing plants with them—one of the great benefits of gardening.

# Index

~

**A**
*Achillea*, 6, 49, 167, 170, 194
   and the I Ching, 33
   as a lawn substitute, 33
   legends and lore of, 31–34
   medicinal properties of, 33
   self-propagation aspect of, 33
*Achillea ageratifolia*, 31
*Achillea borealis*, 32
*Achillea* 'Coronation Gold,' 32, 196
*Achillea millefolium*, 31
*Achillea* 'Moonshine," 32
Achillea 'Paprika,' 32
*Achillea taygetea*, 31
*Achillea wilzekii*, 31
*Adiantum jordanii*, 156
*Aeonium*, 63
*Aeonium* 'Zwartkop,' 63
agave, 62. *See also* century plant
alliums, variegated-leafed, 75
aloe resin, 47
*Aloe vera*, 47, 49
*Aloysia triphylla*, 39
*Alternatives au gazon*, 161
alum root, island, 166
amaryllis, 61
American Bamboo Society, 90
*A Modern Herbal*, 43
anise, 49–50
apartment gardening, 132–135
   and microclimates
   designing of, 132
   indoors, 132
   outdoors, 132
aphids, and oleander, 87

apple tree, 121
apricot tree, 121–122
*Aptenia cordifolia*, 62
*Armeria maritima*, 6–7, 170
*Artemesia dracunculus*, 50
*Artemesia pyncocephala*, 169
Arum family, and contact
   dermatitis, 179
*Arundinaria* genus, 89
*Aquilegia formosa*, 3
*Arbutus unedo*, 6
*Arctostaphylos*, 5
*Asarum caudatum*, 93
asparagus, 122
*Asteraceae*, 162
asters, 14, 163, 164
   and allergies, 178
Audubon, John James, 2
azalea, 143, 147, 150
   wild, 93

**B**
baby blue-eyes, 187
Babylonia, ancient, 131
*Baccharis* genus, 83–85
*Baccharis pilularis*, 84
   Dwarf Chaparral Broom, 84
   Dwarf/Prostrate Coyote Bush, 84
   'Twin Peaks,' 84
   'Pigeon Point,' 84
bamboo, 89–91, 140
   Buddha's Belly, 90–91
   Chinese Goddess, 91
   clumping, 89, 90

~ Index ~

bamboo (continued)
   heavenly, 80, 150
   invasive, 89, 90
   pests of, 91
   propagating of, 91
   running, 89, 90
*Bambusa* genus, 990
*Bambusa multiplex* 'Alphonse Karr,' 90
*Bambusa multiplex riviereorum*, 91
*Bambusa oldhamii*, 90
*Bambusa ventricosa*, 90
barberries, spiny, 80–82
   as a deer repellent, 80
   as a medicinal herb, 80
   Darwin, 81
   Japanese, 81
   magenta-leaved, 149
   maroon, 140
Bartram, John, 100
basil, 47, 49, 125, 164
bay, 49
*Bay Area Gardening*, 93
beehives
   assembling of, 19
   buying of, 19
beekeepers, community of, 22
beekeeping, 14
   and honey extraction process, 21
   backyard, 20–22
   beginning, 17–19
   buying a hive, 17–18
*Beekeeping For Dummies*, 17, 18, 20
"Bee Pastures, The," 162
bees, 162, 163
   African, 13
   and colony collapse, 162
   honey, 13, 17–19
   Italian, 18, 19
   native, 14
   plants that they love, 15

bees (continued)
   Russian, 18
   solitary, 162, 163
Berberidaceae, family, 80
*Berberis darwinii*, 81
*Berberis thunbergii* 'Atropurpurea', 81
*Berberis thunbergii* 'Cherry Bomb', 81–82
*Berberis thunbergii* 'Crimson Pygmy', 82
*Berberis wilsoniae*, 81
   as a medicinal herb, 81
*Berberis* genus, 80–82
Beziers, France,, 161
Bible, the, 99
bindweed, 173
birch, and allergies, 178
Bird, Richard, 40
bishop's hat, 80
Blackiston, Howard, 17
blue dicks, 71
*Book of Herb Lore, The*, 43
borage, 49, 50
*Borago officinalis*, 50
botrytis, 105
bougainvillea, 126, 140
boxwood, 136
Brinker, David, 184
*Brodiaea*, 70, 71
*Brodiaea nana*, 71
*Brodiaea californica*, 71
bromeliads, 61
broom (aggressive, invasive), 76, 173, 190
buckwheat, California, 163
*Buddleia*, 7
bulbs, 173
   California native, 70–72
   creeping rhizomatous, 71
burning, for seed pretreatment, 189

~ Index ~

buttercup, Bermuda, 191
butterflies, 6–7, 147, 162
   and ceanothus, 74
   and rosemary, 24
   habitat for, 10
   larvae of, 7
"butterflies-in-the-wind," 170
butterfly bush, 7
button bush, 164

C
cacti, 60
calandrinia, 163
California Dutchman's pipe, 10
California Invasive Plant Inventory, 66
*California Master Gardener Handbook*, 86, 178, 182
California native bulbs, in autumn, 70–72. *See also* bulbs
California Native Plant Society (Merritt College), 77, 166
*Calochortus albus*, 70–71
*Calochortus amabilis*, 71
carob trees, 95–96
Carlos IV (King), 39
Carmel Creeper, 169
carrots, allergies to, 178
cassia. *See* senna leaf
catmint, 167
Cassia tree, 95
catnip herb, 46
catnip (Nepeta), 137
Ceanothus, 143, 163, 165, 169
*Ceanothus arboreus*, 74, 74
*Ceanothus* blue, 74–76
   attraction for hummingbirds, 74
   for erosion control, 75
   prostrate, 75
   susceptibilities to pests, 76

*Ceanothus griseus horizontalis* 'Carmel Creeper," 74, 75, 169
*Ceanothus hearstiorum*, 75, 165, 169
ceanothus stem gall moth, 76
*Ceanothus thyrsiflorus* 'Skylark,' 75
*Ceanothus tingids*, 76
cedar trees, allergies to, 178
celery, allergies to, 178
*Centhranthus ruber*, 192
Central Arid Zone Research Institute (Jodhpur, India), 110
Central Valley (California), 14–15
century plant, 52
   and dermatitis, 179
chamomile, 49, 50
Channel Islands (California), 3, 32, 166
Chateaudun, France, historical herb garden of, 49
cherry tree, 96
*Chimonobambusa* genus, 89
Chinese apples, 99
Chinese Medicinal Herb Farm (Petaluma, CA), 123
chrysanthemums, 147
   allergies to, 178
*Chusquea* genus, 90
*Cistus* plant, 160
citronelle, 126
citrus tree, 153
*Clarkia*, 187
clay, 181–183
claytonia, 163
clematis, 7
climate change, global, 128
coffeeberry, 93
Cohen, Gail, 116
cold stratification, for seed pretreatment, 189
Collison, Peter, 100
colony collapse disorder, 13, 21, 162

199

## ~ Index ~

columbine, western, 3, 164
*Complete Garden Guide to the Native Shrubs of California*, 84
*Complete Garden Guide to the Native Perennials of California*, 78, 84, 188
*Complete Herbal, The*, 43
compost, 181–182
Connelly, Kevin, 189
coral bells, 3
coral heads, in a garden landscape, 139
coral reef, inspiration from, 139–141
coreopsis, 137
corms, 70
corn plants, 133
cosmos, 6, 7, 164
cotoneaster, sprawling, 149
cotton, lavender, 167
cowslip, and dermatitis, 179
coyote bush, 83–85, 137
*Crocosmia crocosmiiflora*, 6, 194, 196
crown rot, 156, 165
Crusades, the, 50
cucumber, and dermatitis, 179
Culpeper, Nicholas, 43
currants, flowering, 3
cyclamen, 57–59
   caring for, 59
   foliage of, 58
   medicinal uses for, 58–59
   wild, 57
*Cyclamen graecum*, 57
*Cyclamen graecum* 'Glyfada,' 58
*Cyclamen hederifolium* 'Silver Cloud,' 58
*Cyclamen persicum*, 57–58
*Cyclamen purpurascens*, 58, 59
Cyclamen Society, 57

**D**

daisies
   Santa Barbara, 137, 163, 167, 192, 195
   Shasta, 6, 7
dandelion leaf, 46
dandelions, 173
dates, 109–111. *See also* jujube trees
   black, 109
   honey, 109
   medicinal uses for, 109–110, 111
   red, 109
daylilies, 138, 194
   bronze, 137, 166, 194
   'Cranberry Baby,' 194
   'Kelly's Girl,' 194
   'Nile Crane,' 194
   yellow, 140, 166, 194
deadheading, 33, 55, 149
de Dunois, Jean, 49
deer
   foiling them gracefully, 148–150
   resistance, 155
Demeter, 99
de Parma, Maria Luisa, 39
dermatitis, from garden plants, 178, 179, 180
   treatment for, 179–180
developments, housing, 15
*Dichelostemma*s, 71
*Dichelostemma*s *capitatum*, 71
*Dichelostemma*s *ida-maia*, 71
*Dichelostemma*s *multiflorum*, 71
*Dietes*, 75, 138, 169, 195
diffenbachia, and dermatitis, 179
Dioscorides (Greek surgeon), 58
dividing, 32, 70, 194–196
drip system, 8, 11, 147
drought, 128, 159. See also water, shortages
drought-resistant plants, 159

200

## ~ Index ~

"Dry Garden Practice and Philosophy, The," 159
*Dryopteris arguta*, 158

**E**
earthworms, 182
*Echeveria*, 62
*Echeveria* 'Blue Curl,' 62
*Echeveria secunda*, 62
*Echinacea*, 14
*Echium*, 150
eggplant, 122
Emery, Dara E., 189
*Energetics of Western Herbs, The*, 81
energy usage, 128
entryways, aromatic, 125–127
*Epilobium*, 4, 6, 79, 81
*Epilobium canum*, 78, 191
*Epimedium*, 80
epiphytes, 61
*Equisetum hyemale*, 7
Erigeron, 137, 192, 195
*Erigeron karvinskianus*, 167, 192
*Euphorbia*, 64–66
    attributes of, 64
    medicinal properties of, 64
    succulents of, 64
*Euphorbia amygdaloides* var. *robbiae*, 65–66
*Euphorbia amygdaloides purpurea*, 66
*Euphorbia characias*, 65
*Euphorbia characias wulfenii*, 64
*Euphorbia characias characias*, 64
*Euphorbia esuta*, 66
*Euphorbia oblongata*, 66
*Euphorbia terracina*, 66
evergreens, 139
    black pine, 143
    mugo pine, 143

**F**
fairy lanterns, fragile, 70

*Fargesia genus*, 90
ferns, 143
    bracken
    asparagus, 133, 134, 148
    California, 156
    California gold back, 157
    California wood, 158
    bird's foot, 156
    coffee, 156
    drought-tolerant, 155–158
    hummingbird, 5
    leather leaf, 157
    licorice, 158
    maidenhair, 133
    sword, 75, 93, 155, 156, 158, 194, 196
    terms useful in describing, 156
fertilizers, 11
    runoff of, 128
fescue, blue, 140
*Ficus benjamina*, 133
*Ficus*, genus, 103, 179
fig canker, 105
fig trees, 7, 103–105
    Brown Turkey, 103
    Golden, 103
    history of, 103
    Kadota, 103
    Mission, 103
    roots of, 104, 105
    Sierra, 103
    Tiger, 103
    varieties of, 103
Filippi, Olivier, 159, 161
firecracker flower, 71
fireweed, 79
food, as medicine, 121–123
    Chinese medicinal, 121, 122–123
    vegetables, 122
    western medicinal, 122
    yang foods, 121

~ Index ~

food, as medicine (continued)
  yin foods, 121
foxglove, and dermatitis, 179
*Fragaria californica*, 166, 191
fronds, 156
fruit fly, Mediterranean, 107
fuchsia (California native), 4, 6
  California, 77, 78, 191–192
fuchsia, hummingbird, 4

**G**
*Galvezia speciosa*, 5
*Gardener's Guide to California Wildflowers*, 189
*Gardening With a Wild Heart*, 37, 76, 78, 83, 187
gardens
  and deer resistance, 148–150
  apartment, 132–135. *See also* apartment gardening
  bones of, 136
  habitat, 7, 9, 74
  Greek, 88
  meadow-style, 6
  rain, 184–186
  rooftop container garden in Greece, 145–147
  sustainable, 9–12
  urban, 15
  wildlife-friendly, 9–11
  without watering, 159–161
garlic
  allergies to, 178
  as a superior herb, 123
  society, 7
Gattefosse (French father of aromatherapy), 43
gaura, 7
*Gaura lindheimeri*, 170
geophytes, 60
*Georgics*, 43
geraniums, 136, 147

(geraniums, continued)
  ivy, 54–56
  rose-scented, 6, 126
  vining, 134
Gibbons, Euell, 34
*Gilia*, 187
gilia, white, 163
ginger
  allergies to, 178
  wild, 93
gladioli, salmon, 138
Golden Gate Canyon (Colorado), 148
Golden Gate Park (San Francisco), 144
goldenrod, 46
grapes, growing of, 115-117
  and wine production, 116
  arbors for, 115–116
  Concord, 116
  table, 116
grasses, 14
  Bermuda, 173
  blue-eyed, 169
  blue fescue, 140
  bronze fountain, 140
  ornamental, 153
  pampas, as an invasive, 190
  straw-colored, 140
  yellow-eyed, 169
grevillea bush, 138, 140, 149, 164, 167
*Grevillea* 'Canberra', 5
*Grevillea rosmarinifolia*, 167
Grieves, Mrs. M., 1931 treatise of, 43
*Growing Native California Plants*, 84, 188
guava, 112–114
  as a medicinal herb, 113
  Brazilian, 113
  bushes, 122

202

## ~ Index ~

guava (continued)
   lemon, 113
   origins of, 112
   species of, 113
   strawberry, 113
   tropical, 113

**H**
habitat, increasing wild, 15
Hacone Japanese Garden (Saratoga, CA), 143–144
Hagar, Edward, 111
Hanging Gardens of Babylon, 128
hardscaping, 136
Havel, Virginia, 93
Hearst Castle, 75, 165, 169
*Hemerocallus*, 166, 194
*Hemizonia* species, 163
hens and chicks, 62
Herbes de Provence, 43
herbicides, 177
herbs, aromatic, 125
herbs, Chinese medicinal, 45–48
   as diuretics, 46
   as expectorants, 47
   as laxatives, 46–47
   superior, 123
   to promote sweating, 45–46
herbs
   growing of in one pot, 134
   growing on kitchen windowsill, 133–134
   with history, 49–52
*Heuchera maxima*, 3, 166
hollyhocks, 6, 7
Holmes, Peter, 81
horsetail, 7
Houdret, Jessica, 40
"How to Build Concord Grape Arbors," 116
huckleberry, 93
hummingbirds, 9, 167

hummingbirds (continued)
   blooms to attract, 2–5, 6, 74, 77
Hummingbird Trumpet, 77
hyacinths, 61, 124
   wild, 71
hyssop, 164

**I**
inside-out flower, 80
invasives, 190–193
   exotic, 190
   Mediterranean species, 192–193
   native (California), 190, 191–192
iris, 70, 143
   African, 149, 169, 195
   California native, 70
   Douglas, 70, 166
   Gladwin, 194, 196
   Pacific Coast, 70
   Pacific Coast Hybrids (PCH), 70, 166
*Iris douglasiana*, 70, 166
Isis, 99
Isle of Wight, and lemon verbena, 39
Ithuriel's spear and milk lily, 71
ivy, and living walls, 130
   Swedish, 130, 133
ivy
   English, allergies to, 178
   poison, 178

**J**
jade plant, 60
Japanese Garden
   San Blas Islands, Panama, 139, 140
   destinations in, 142
   elements of in garden design, 142
   pathways in, 142
   sculptures in, 142

Japanese Garden (continued)
   tranquility in, 142–144
   water features in, 142, 143
*Japanese Garden Design*, 89
Japanese Friendship Garden (San Jose), 144
Japanese Tea Garden (San Francisco), 144
Jefferson, Thomas, 99
Jekyll, Gertrude (garden designer), 65
Joan of Arc, 49
Juba II, King of Numidia, 64
jujube trees, 109–111
   cultivars of, 110
   'Land,' 110
   'Li,' 110
   origins of, 109
   'So,' 110
   'Topeka,' 110
junipers, 139, 143, 148

**K**
Keane, Marc P., 89
Keator, Glenn, 37, 84, 188
Kirk, Donald, 158
*Kitchen and Herb Gardener, The*, 40
kiwi vines, male and female, 122
Kloss, Jethro, 28
*Kniphofia uvaria*, 4, 167, 194, 196
Koran, the, 99

**L**
lace bug, 76
lambs ears, wooly, 7
landscaping, sustainable, 128
Larner, Judith, 187
Larner Seeds, 83
*Lavendula*, 7
*Lavendula angustifolia*, 29
*Lavendula dentata*, 29
*Lavendula intermedia* 'Provence,' 29, 30

*Lavendula stoechas*, 27
lavender, 27–30, 39, 49, 81, 138, 140, 194
   as aromatic herb, 125, 126
   as one of Herbes de Provence, 43
   benefits of for insects and birds, 29
   benefits of pruning of, 28
   English, 7, 29, 30
   French, 7, 29, 30, 137
   lemonade, recipe for, 28
   Spanish, 27, 30, 149, 150, 163
   use of in cooking, 28
   use of in Elizabethan times, 28
   use of in Roman times, 28
   wands, 29
   water required for, 27
leaflets, 156
lemon, 49
   balm, 49, 51–52
   verbena, as aromatic herb, 125
   trees, 147
*Levisticum officinale*, 51
light, amount of in garden, 152
lilacs, California wild, 169
lilies, 163
   calla, 150
   California native, 71–72, 163
   creamy mariposa, 70, 71
   fortnight, 75, 149, 169, 194, 195
   harvest, 71
   Humboldt, 72
   leopard, 71
*Lilium humboldtii*, 72
*Lilium pardalinum*, 72
Linnaeus, Carolus, 64
lily-of-the-valley, 93
lily turf, 143
Litchfield, Ken, 118, 119, 120
lobelia, 137
lovage, 49, 51

~ Index ~

Low Impact Development, 185
Lowry, Judith, 37, 76, 78, 83
LuAnn, garden of, 6–8
lupine, 164, 187

**M**

magnolias, allergies to, 178
*Maianthemum dilatatum*, 93
manzanita, 5, 7, 164
marigolds, 140
Marin County, California, 54, 57, 59, 83, 96, 100, 106, 107, 127, 139, 148
marjoram, 164
Master Gardener course, 152
*Matricaria recutita*, 50
McGegor, Mr., garden of, 50
meditation, 143
Mediterranean Garden Society (Athens, Greece), 159
Mediterranean Sea, 145
*Melissa officinalis*, 51–52
*Mentha spicata*, 192–193
*Mentha piperita*, 45
Meyer, Frank, 110
Meyer, Roger, 110
microclimates, 56
    and disease in plants, 153
    and light, 153
    and moisture, 153
    and slope, 153
    and wind, 153
    in an apartment, 132–133
    in the garden, 152–154
Mid-Winter Exposition (1894), 144
milkweed, 10, 179
*Mimulus aurantiacus*, 4, 166, 169
*Mimulus guttatus*, 169
mint, 49, 163, 192–193
    and deer resistance, 149
    peppermint leaf, 45–46
mites, parasitic, 13, 18

Monemvasia (Byzantine fortress town), 62
monkey flower, 4, 163, 166
    sticky, 169
montbretia, 6
mother-in-law's tongue, 61
*Mountains of California, The*, 162
Muir Beach, 168
Muir, John, 162
    "sweet bee garden" of, 164
mulching, 168
multiplying, 194–196
Mu Qi, 96
mushrooms, 118–120
    blewits, 120
    coral, 120
    garden giant, 120
    giant morels, 120
    mycelium, 118
    oyster, 120
    shaggy manes, 120
Mycological Society of San Francisco, 118

**N**

*Nandina*, 80, 150
narcissus
    allergies to, 178
    paper white, 134
"Native Plants Under Redwoods," 93
natives, drought-resistant, in California, 162–164
    replacement of by crops, 162
*Native Shrubs of California*, 37
Neolithic Period, and Egyptians, 115
*Nepita*, 46
*Nepita faassenii*, 167
Northcote, Lady Rosalind, 43
nutsedge, 173

## ~ Index ~

**O**
oak, poison, 173, 178
oak root
   fungus, 156
   rot, 165
oak tree, 150, 155
   California live, 165, 168
   coast live, 156, 165
   planting under, 165–167
   Valley, 156, 168
*Ocimum basilicum*, 47
oleander, 86–88, 146, 147, 150
   allergies to, 178
   dwarf varieties of, 88
   gall, 88
   history of, 86–87
   hybrids, 88
   poisonous nature of, 86
olives
   Athenas, 106
   Chalkidiki, 106
   "donkey," 106
   farm of in Greece, 106, 117, 126
   fertilization of, 107
   Gaidero, 106, 107
   Kalamata, 106, 107
   Koroneiki, 106
   processing for table, 107–108
   table, 106–108
   trees, 106–108, 147
onions
   allergies to, 178
   green, 122
orange peel, mandarin, as a superior herb, 123
orchids, 134
oregano, 39, 49
   as an aromatic herb, 125, 126
Osiris, 99
Osterman, Joseph, 87
*Otatea* genus, 90
over-watering, 165

*Oxalis*, 73
*Oxalis oregana*, 93, 191
*Oxalis pexcaprae* (formerly *O. cernua*), 191
oyster shell scale, 76

**P**
palms, curly-leafed, 133
pansies, 140
parsley, and dermatitis, 179
parsnip, and dermatitis, 179
Pasalimani (harbor near Piraeus, Greece), 147
pathos, and allergies, 179
Payne, Theodore, 187
*Pelargonium graveolens*, 6, 126
*Pelargonium peltatum*, 54–56
*Pelargonium* genus, 134
*Pellaea andromedifolia*, 156
*Pellaea mucronata*, 156
Peloponnese, southern (Greece), 57
*Penstemon*, 6, 7
penstemon, firebird, 4
*Penstemon gloxiniodes*, 5
*Pentagramma triangularis*, 157
pepper tree, 7
Persephone, 99
Persian violet, 58
persimmon tree, 96
pesticides, 7, 11, 13, 15
   and toxicity, 128, 162
Peter Rabbit, 50
petunias, 140
phacelia, 164
philodendron, and dermatitis, 179
photinia, 146, 147
*Phyllostachys* genus, 89
*Phytophthora* genus, water mold, 74, 176
*Pimpinella anisum*, 49–50
pincushion flowers, 164

## ~ Index ~

pine tree, 150
    allergies to, 178
    Monterey, 9, 152
pinnae, 156
Piraeus, Greece, 145
planters, and living walls, 131
*Planting Design for Dry Gardens*, 161
planting, in layers, 136–138
    and hardscaping, 136
    horizontal or vertical, 136
Plant Introduction Station (Chico, CA), 110
plants, poisonous, in garden, 178–180
Pliny, information about thyme, 43
*Podocarpus*, 150
poinsettias, 64, 179
poker plants, red hot, 4, 167, 194
pollinators
    and California's almond crop, 17
    how to help, 13–16
pollution
    air, 128
    water, 128
*Polypodium glycyrrhiza*, 158
*Polypodium scouleri*, 157
*Polystichum munitum*, 155, 158
pomegranates, 99–102
    Balegal, 100
    Cloud, 100
    Crab, 100
    cultivars of, 100
    cultivation instructions for, 100
    dwarf, 100
    Early Wonderful, 100–101
    Fleshman, 101
    Granada, 101
    Greek, 99
    Green Globe, 101
    Home, 101

pomegranates (continued)
    in history, 99
    in mythology, 99
    juice of, 101
    King, 101
    Phoenicia, 101
poor man's orchid, 58
poppies, California, 27, 137, 150, 163, 187
potato vine, 146
    purple, 7
Potter, Beatrix, 59
*Pour un jardin sans arrosage*, 161
Presidio Community Garden, 118, 119
Pride of Madeira, 150
primrose, allergies to, 178
Prince George's County (Maryland), 184
*Pseudomonas syringae* pv. Savastanoi, 88
*Psidium cattleianum*, 113
*Psidium cattleianum* 'Sabine', 113
*Psidium cattleianum* spp. *lucidum Degener*, 113
*Psidium guajava*, 113
*Psidium guineense*, 113
*Pteridium aquilinum*, 157
*Pythium fungi*, 176

**Q**

Quarryhill Botanical Garden (Glen Ellen, CA), 123
*qi*, concept of, 45, 46, 47
*Quercus agrifolia*, 156, 168
*Quercus lobata*, 156, 168

**R**

"rain gardens," 184–186
redbud, California, 164
redwoods, 155
    'Adpressa,' 94

~ Index ~

redwoods (continued)
    and root rot
    'Aptos Blue," 94
    as garden plants, 92–94
    burls of, 94
    coast, 92
    cultivars of, 94
    'Filoli,' 94
    'Prostrata,' 94
    'Santa Cruz,' 94
    'Soquel,' 94
    survival techniques of, 94
    'Woodside,' 94
resources, non-renewable, 128
*Rhamnus californica*, 93
rhizomes, 70, 77, 89, 173
rhododendron, 143, 150, 160
*Rhododendron occidentale*, 93
*Rhus* genus, allergies to, 178
*Ribes malvaceum*, 3
*Ribes sanguineum*, 3
roofs, green, 128–130
    benefits of, 128–130
root rot, 94, 176
roots
    depth of, 159
    developing long, straight, 160, 161
    "roots versus shoots," 160
root-to-shoot ratio, 160–161
rosemary, 7, 24–26, 39, 49, 81, 147, 149, 164, 194, 195
    as aromatic herb, 125
    as medicinal and culinary herb, 24
    propagation of, 25
    prostrate, 138, 140, 167
    Tuscan, 136, 140
    uses for, 26
roses, 7, 67–69
    and good garden hygiene, 68
    bare root, 67, 68

roses (continued)
    before planting, 69
    bushes, 6
    choosing, 68
    need for sun, 67
    propagation of, 25
    pruning of, 68
    rock, 160
    tending to in January, 67–69
    tree, 6
    wild, 164
Rosmarinus 'Huntington Blue," 167
*Rosmarinus officinalis*, 24
*Rosmarinus officinalis* 'Huntington Carpet,' 25
*Rosmarinus officinalis* 'Prostatus,' 24, 125, 146
*Rosmarinus officinalis* 'Tuscan Blue,' 25
*Rumex acetosa*, 50–51
*Rumex scutatus*, 51
runoff, rain, rerouting, 184–186

**S**

sage, 49, 51. *See also Salvia*
    autumn, 4, 6, 37
    black, 37
    Cleveland's, 36, 37
    creeping, 37
    hummingbird, 37
    pineapple, 36
    purple bush, 6
    Mexican, 4, 36, 137, 195
    Sandhill, 169
*Salvia*, 35–38, 163, 194
    belonging to the mint family Lamiaceae, 35
    bushes, 152
*Salvia clevelandii*, 3, 4, 36, 37, 137, 152, 163, 168
*Salvia elegans*, 36

## ~ Index ~

*Salvia greggii*, 4, 6, 37, 137
*Salvia leucantha*, 4, 6, 36, 195
*Salvia mellifera*, 37
*Salvia offinalis*, 35, 51
    as a medicinal and culinary herb, 35, 36
*Salvia sonomensis*, 36, 37
*Salvia spathacea*, 37
*Salvia splendens*, 35
*Salvia uliginosa*, 36
San Francisco Bay gardening, 158, 184
San Mateo Japanese Garden, 144
San Pablo Bay, California, 49, 142
sansevieria, 61. *See also* snake plant *and* mother-in-law's tongue
*Santolina chamaecyparissus*, 167
Santolinas, 81, 149
    silvery-leaved, 137
scarification, 189
Schafer, Peg, 123
Schmidt, Marjorie, 84, 188
Scottish Highlands, and thyme, 44
sea ink, 6
sedum, 6
    and green roofs, 129
seedbed, creating a weed-free, 187
*Seed Propagation of Native California Plants*, 189
seeds, sowing of, 187–189
    components of seed handling, 188
    pretreatment of, 188–189
    wildflower, 187
*Senna acutifolia*, 46
*Senna angustifolia*, 46
senna leaf, 46
*Sequoia sempervirens*, 92
*Sisyrinchium bellum*, 169
*Sisyrinchium californicum*, 169
"Six Persimmons" (painting), 96

snake plant, 61
snapdragon, island bush, 65
snow-in-the-summer, 7
soil
    and pore space, 181, 182
    clay, thriving in, 168–170
    drainage, 181–183
    four principle components of, 182
    health of, 128
    loam, 181
    potting, 182–183
    sand, 181
*Solanum*, 146
*Solidago*, 46
Solomon, 99
Sonoma County, California, 92
sori, 156
sorrel, 49, 50–51
    common, 50–51
    French, 51
    redwood, 93, 191
    wood (*Oxalis*), 173
spurge, Mediterranean, 64, 65
    cultivars of, 65
    'Ember Queen,' 65
    'Humpty Dumpty,' 65
    'Jade Dragon,' 65
    'John Tomlinson,' 65
*Stachys*, 7
*Stalking the Healthful Herbs*, 34
stolons, 173
Strawberry Festival, 76
strawberry
    trees, 6
    woodland, 150, 163, 166, 191
succulents, low-water, 60–63
    attributes helping them conserve water, 61
    stem, 60
sumac, poison, 178
sunflower, 164

~ Index ~

**T**
Tamalpais, Mount, 190
Tam, Mount, 169
*Taraxacum officinale*, 46
tarragon, 49
    French, 50
tarweed, 163
thatch, 175
thrift, common, 170
thyme, 42–44, 47, 49
    common, 42
    creeping, 42
    essential part of Herbes de Provence, 43
    'Herbe Baronne,' 42
    history of, 43–44
    honey, 43
    lemon, 42
    preference for sun and dry, sandy soil, 44
    wild, 42, 43
    woolly, 42, 137, 150
thymol (active ingredient in thyme), 43
    use of by Egyptians, 43
    use of by Sumerians, 43
*Thymus citriodoris*, 42
*Thymus herba-barona*, 42
*Thymus lanuginosus*, 42
*Thymus serpyllum*, 42
*Thymus vulgaris*, 42, 47
Tiburon, California, 74
tidy-tips, 187
tomatoes, 153, 179
tough love, for plants, 159
toyon tree, 150
trees, specimen, 95–97
*Trileleias*, 71
trillium, 70
trimming, 161
tubers, 173
tulips, 70

tulips (continued)
    bulbs of, and allergies, 178
    globe, 70
turnips, and dermatitis, 179

**U**
University of California Botanical Garden, 45, 144

**V**
*Vaccinium ovatum*, 93
valerian, 49, 137, 140, 192
*Vancouveria*, 80
verbena, dark purple, 137, 163
verbena, lemon, 39–41, 125, 126
    need of for sunlight, 41
    uses of, 40–41
*Viburnum*, genus, 104
*Vinca minor*, 150
vines, and living walls, 130
*Viola sempervirens*, 93
violet, 162
    redwood, 93
Virgil, 43
von Humboldt, Baron Alexander, 35
Vossen, Paul, 116

**W**
walls, living, 128–131
    benefits of, 128–129, 130–131
water
    conservation, 9
    gardening without, 159–161
    hot, for seed pretreatment, 189
    shortages, 128
    storm water management, 128
watering schedule, 8
weeding, by hand, 12
weeds, identification and control of, 172–177
    and irrigation, 175

## ~ Index ~

weeds (continued)
   and mulch, 176
   and soil, 174–175
   annuals, 172–173
   barriers for, 176
   biennials, 173
   broadleaf (dicots), 173
   chemical, 177
   control of, 174–176
   cultural, 174
   definition of, 172
   grasses (monocot), 173
   identification of, 172–174
   mechanical, 175–176
   perennials, 173
   physical, 176
*Wild Edible Plants*, 158
willow, 164
wine apples, 99
wine, grapes for, 116

## X
xeriscape, 11

## Y
yarrow, 31–34, 167, 170
   brick-red, 6
   common names of, 31
   Greek, 31
   value of in healing wounds, 31, 33–34
yerba Buena, 7
yew, 150
yucca, 160

## Z
*Zauschneria* (aka *Epilobium*), 77–79, 163. *See also* fuchsia, California
   and self-propagation, 77
   attractive to birds, 77
*Zauschneria californica*, 4, 6, 77, 78, 191. *See also Epilobium*
*Zauschneria latifolium*, 77, 78
Zauschner, Johann Baptista Josef, 79
zinnias, 140
*Ziziphus jujuba*, 109

# About the Author

~

Barbara J. Euser writes about gardening and travel. Her articles and essays have appeared in magazines and anthologies. She wrote *Take 'Em Along, Somaliland, Children of Dolpo*, and the children's book *The Neighbor and the Stone*. She coauthored *Golf in Greece* and *Golf in Italy*. She edited gardening anthologies *Bay Area Gardening* and *Gardening Among Friends* and travel anthologies *A Climber's Climber, Floating through France, Venturing in Southern Greece, Venturing in Ireland*, and *Venturing in Italy*. She is a retired lawyer and former political officer with the Foreign Service of the U.S. Department of State. As a director of the International Community Development Foundation, she has worked on projects in Bosnia, Somaliland, Zimbabwe, Nepal and Nicaragua.

www.ingramcontent.com/pod-product-compliance
Lightning Source LLC
LaVergne TN
LVHW090115080426
835507LV00040B/868